Exploring the Landscape of the Mind

Exploring the Landscape of the Mind

An Introduction to Psychodynamic Therapy

Janet Lee Bachant, Ph.D.

IPBOOKS.net
International Psychoanalytic Books

International Psychoanalytic Books (IPBooks)
New York • http://www.IPBooks.net

Published by International Psychoanalytic Books (IPBooks)
Queens, New York
Online at: www.IPBooks.net

Book cover design by Janet Lee Bachant

Interior book design by Medlar Publishing Solutions Pvt Ltd., India

www.IPBooks.net

ISBN: 978-1-949093-36-0

For Miriam and Rod

Table of Contents

Part III

Therapeutic Skills: Listening for the Footprints of the Past

Part IV

Changing How Patients Relate to Childhood Trauma and Adversity

Acknowledgments

This book could not have been written without the courage and generosity of my patients who have given me permission to share their journeys into the unknown territories of their inner lives. To them I owe a debt of gratitude that can never be repaid. Thank you for your perseverance, fortitude and desire to breathe life into processes that would be a pale shadow of the intimate landscape without your help.

Bessel Van der Kolk and Judith Herman read, commented upon and made useful suggestions to parts of the book that enhanced my thinking and perspective. Thank you. A special acknowledgement is reserved for Jim Levin whose collaboration and vision enriched my writing.

Special thanks are also due to dear friends Helen and Elliot Adler who sustained me through many years of developing my thinking, providing me with friendship and feedback that made the book better. I am indebted to Elliot for his openness to my using our book, *Working in Depth: Framework and Flexibility in the Analytic Relationship* as a foundation for my thinking and as a touchstone for developing my own ideas. Arthur Lynch,

Arnie and Arlene Richards, Emel and Sagman Kayatakin patiently read through earlier sections of the manuscript, giving me honest, critical and incisive feedback. To Tong Jun and Wu Zhilly I am grateful for opportunities to teach and meet students whose questions and comments have been a vital part of the development of my thinking. My students have significantly enhanced my ability to articulate what is at the heart of the therapeutic process. I am grateful also to my ongoing study group in Guangzhou, and especially to David Zhang, for continued opportunities to organize and explore my ideas.

I am grateful that my psychoanalytic education was at an eclectic institute, The Westchester Center for Psychoanalysis and Psychotherapy, where I was exposed to a broad range of dynamic thinking that influenced my development as a therapist. Thank you WCSPP!

Jonathan Shedler, Marsha Wineburgh, Ruth Greer, Chantal Clevenot, Roy Wallace, Lynne Rubin, and Loretta Hayes read parts of the book and gave me encouragement in the process. Martin Bergman helped me to develop firsthand a conviction about the value and importance of free association and the ability to listen on many levels.

To the team at IP Books, Matthew Bach, Kathy Kovacic, and Larry Schwartz, I owe thanks for their useful suggestions, commentary and help with the cover. Special acknowledgement goes to Sylvain Durand whose mentoring, expertise and guidance in Photoshop made the cover come alive.

Finally, I am lovingly indebted to Georges Millet who always has my back and who has unfailingly encouraged me and supported my work in countless ways.

Introduction

Psychotherapy is an adventure into uncharted territory — the landscape of the mind. As therapists, beginning a treatment takes us on a journey into the unmapped interior of a person's soul. We do not know what awesome vistas, formidable obstacles and strange inhabitants we will encounter. But we do know that the exploration of the self is the path to finding answers to some of life's greatest personal mysteries such as How did I become the person I am? How can I address the mystery of my problems in living? What do I really want? Who am I? Psychodynamic treatment is akin to the great voyages of discovery in which significant dangers are faced but the rewards of discovery outweigh the difficulties of the journey (Levin, 2017). On all such encounters, each participant has a necessary role to play as they together embark on an adventure that has no equal.

Uncovering complex mental processes (many of which are unconscious) in the context of an ongoing, intimate relationship is the core of psychodynamic therapy. It demands intellectual understanding, emotional connectedness and, ideally, a sense of humor to help keep things in perspective. Doing psychotherapy tests patient and therapist alike, asking them both to deal with fears, tensions, losses, limitations, exposure and maintaining a focus on the growing edge of development through the inevitable setbacks and disappointments. But it also provides an arena for authentic relatedness and a commitment to the collaborative work of knowing a person's internal life. The potential for understanding generated by psychotherapy is unrivaled. Shedler (2010) reports the recurring finding that "the benefits of psychodynamic therapy not only endure but increase with time" in contrast to non-dynamic therapies whose gains decay over time (p. 102–103). In the words of students who have captured the essence succinctly: "It goes deeper." "It goes to the heart."

The primary function of this book is to help the reader begin a voyage of discovery. While everyone's path will be different, there are steps each of us can take to understand the minds of others and thereby to organize our own as therapists. The techniques developed in this book focus primarily on the ordinary processes of mental organization, processes that are determined by the interaction of biological, emotional and interpersonal factors during the child's early years. In addition to addressing how normal development informs psychodynamic technique, this book also highlights the long-term effects of traumatic emotional experiences on the child's mental functioning.

We must bear in mind that all psychological problems are not caused by trauma. Adversity is not necessarily traumatic, as it can stimulate the emergence of adaptive modes of being, such as helping others or discovering inner strengths. We can think of adverse emotional experiences as occurring along a continuum, where there is considerable variation in how mental life is affected. Given the bio/psycho/social determinants of experience, we keep in mind that even a mode of relating that was intended to be nurturing will not necessarily be organized in the mind of the child in the same way. A mother whose own mother was a "helicopter parent" may intend to give her child the emotional breathing room she didn't have. How the child *interprets* this breathing room, however, will depend on many factors and can run the gamut from a gift of freedom to the experience of detachment or uncaring. The intensity of the adversity and how children understand it will be major considerations in determining whether that experience is traumatizing. Adversity can generate defenses that add value to an individual's functioning, as well as impairing our capacity for love or work.

Traumatic childhood experiences that have pervasive negative effects on development and emotional health are much more common than was originally thought. Van der Kolk (2005) has suggested a broadening of the concept of trauma to include the effects on mental life of the long-term consequences of chronic emotional adversity in childhood on mental development.

Like footprints in wet sand, the meanings children make of adverse childhood experiences leave their mark on psychic organization. Becoming sensitive to the traces of early childhood organization gives us a direct line to the patient's most important issues: the fears, wishes and fantasies that structure their experience but have been mostly split off from awareness. Attachments, strategies, and modes of relating that work well are generally integrated into the normal sense of self and functioning. These dimensions of experience are extremely important in the therapeutic process, providing the indispensable strength and sustenance needed to sustain the challenge of working on change. Split off, disconnected fears and fantasies, however, those set in motion by early traumatic circumstances require more therapeutic attention. The sequelae of these early experiences have been structured by the developing mind into problematic enduring patterns of automatic relating to self and others. Psychotherapists need to understand how the traces of childhood abuse, neglect and disordered attachment are woven into the fabric of the individual's emergent sense of self so that their listening and interventions can be appropriately applied.

This type of complex developmental trauma touches all our lives. Rarely does a treatment *not* have to deal with the deep currents left in the wake of early developmental troubles. From the unavoidable calamities of childhood to the relational trauma of abuse and neglect that challenge many, traces of how these experiences were organized in the child's mind pervade the process of psychotherapy. This book is based on the premise that indicators of how children learn to organize and deal with ordinary childhood experience and trauma are active in every session, offering patient and therapist countless opportunities to work on critical aspects of suffering. Knowing how to listen for the signs of early organization can give us access to underlying processes that structure the patient's mental life. Working with the traces of early organization that are represented in all psychotherapy sessions brings the patient's development into the room, where together patient and therapist can collaborate to identify, examine and work directly on understanding the journey into the interior.

Traumatic distress emerges from any experience that leaves the individual feeling overwhelmed and alone, even if it does not cause physical harm (Freud 1893b). Typically, early trauma is defined as the effect of an event or situation that exceeds the person's resources and ability to cope (James 2008). Although interest in trauma has been with us for more than 100 years, a focus on developmental trauma has come to the center of dynamic thinking only relatively recently. This type of trauma is rooted in the interplay of early interpersonal experience *and how the child perceives that experience.* Brenner (1982) and Viorst (1998) speak of these experiences as the calamities of childhood, the inevitable and necessary losses that we all face in the course of growing up. The most important determinant of childhood emotional trauma is the meaning a child gives to the experience. In contrast to acute trauma, developmental trauma is typically cumulative and consequently complex, shaped by maturational, emotional and defensive efforts to deal with early emotional pain. Van der Kolk's (2013) definition of trauma is most evocative: "not being able to tolerate knowing what you know, seeing what you see" and, I would add, feeling what you feel. Many factors, including the child's long period of dependency and the slow development of the brain, contribute to our understanding that traumatic childhood experiences are pervasive and can have lifelong consequences (Cozolino, 2002; Ginot, 2015; Herman, 1992/1997; Schore, 2015; Van der Kolk, 2005). As Lily, whose childhood history led her to the threshold of suicide, recently commented, "There is nothing more traumatic."

> What best describes Lily's childhood is that whenever her father's car pulled into the driveway, the family dog scrambled desperately to find a hiding place. By the time she was in college, Lily's deep depression and despair had become so overwhelming that she started giving away her possessions in preparation for ending her life. Fortunately, an

aunt noticed that something was radically wrong and referred her to a psychiatrist. With tears and halting words, Lily remembers being in his office telling him that she didn't understand what was wrong with her: she hadn't lost a parent or been sexually abused, but she just didn't want to live. Her psychiatrist took in what she was saying and responded, "You have lost much more. You have lost yourself." That exchange of understanding was the spark that enabled Lily to begin the process of finding her road to recovery from the childhood experiences that almost claimed her life. This journey has taken many years.

Psychological trauma is more than an event for which we are unprepared. It is an event that creates a psychic injury that deeply disturbs one's mental equilibrium. Trauma is very individual. An experience that might be traumatic for one person may be organized by another as a personal challenge having little or no traumatic effects. Trauma is in the eye of the beholder, but our biology also contributes importantly to how we are vulnerable to it. People with a low threshold for anxiety may be more vulnerable to trauma. Physical pain (from injuries or operations, for example), even when the child has psychological support, can have long-lasting psychological consequences. Children, because of the long period of dependence on their caretakers while their minds are still developing and their resources limited, are more much more vulnerable than adults. Children meet the world with immature cognitive functions leaving them more influenced by fantasy and early emotional processing than adults confronting a challenging experience. This is why abuse or neglect of children can have such long-ranging consequences. The wounds created by what is emotionally traumatizing are structured into the child's experience of self and others, into the very heart of relatedness.

This understanding views interpersonal adversity as an inevitable part of being human. We have all experienced at least some of these challenges in our lifetimes. During childhood we are confronted with imperfect attachments, the task of making sense of innumerable losses, and developing a sense of whom we can and cannot trust. To make matters even more complicated, those we learn to be wary of in some ways are the very people we want to turn to in others. Our relationships are inevitably ambivalent, inherently complex. It is the very rare person who does not grow up having experienced some sort of trauma, be it a one-time event, cumulative relational stressors, or lasting, maladaptive beliefs that developed through the fantasies and strategies generated to deal with early emotional difficulties. Childhood abuse, neglect, loss and problematic attachment have enduring consequences. No one escapes childhood unscathed.

Traces of ways of relating that formed through early childhood experience, positive and negative, color everything the patient does and especially how patients relate. We can learn to identify the sequelae of these childhood ways of experiencing, found in every session, to guide our technique. Working with the traces left behind by childhood struggles, losses and conflictual attachments provides us with early intervention techniques that enable us to identify and address the organization of mental functioning *before* the process of emotional hijacking is irreversibly activated. Later in the book we will look at how emotional hijacking can be used therapeutically by examining and working with the inevitable enactments that arise between patients and therapists.

Our primary goal as we start a treatment is working to understand how this patient's mind works. We survey the landscapes of our patient's minds, their mental organization. Most often this means identifying, working on and working through the painful re-emergence of the effects of childhood developmental adversity. Within the context of the calm, safe environment of the therapeutic interaction, an essential component of trauma work (Herman, 1992/1997; Van der Kolk, 2014), traces of these experiences give us the data we need to explore how these early experiences were organized. Maintaining a balanced therapeutic environment, one in which patients have the capacity to reflect on their experience while confronting emotional distress facilitates integration. This reflective process itself changes the patient's relationship to early losses, conflicts, and disordered attachment by facilitating the development of an observing ego and enabling the patient to see and feel what is going on within. Markers of emotional stress can be identified in how we relate to others, how we learned to protect ourselves against early emotional pain as well as in how we relate to *ourselves*. For example, from early emotional neglect or abuse we might learn a characteristic way of disconnecting from ourselves, connecting to others through passive aggressiveness, submitting to authority, and so on. The section *Listening for the Footprints of the Past* gives us the building blocks we need to listen to the patient's narrative as psychotherapists. Developing our ability to address the subtle markers of early forms of organization as represented in the patient's everyday experience provides us with countless opportunities to explore core issues.

Unifying the approach presented in this book is a conscious appreciation of the processes by which traces of traumatic childhood experiences and developmental trauma stimulate emotional activation in the present. Emotional activation of early relatedness can be generated through inner and outer sources.

Interactions with others, sensory activation (the smells, sights, sounds, touches of ordinary living), as well as the constant flow of inner thoughts, feelings and fantasies, reverberate with mental patterns of organization. This arousal can be immediate and intense, activating intense emotion, like rousing a sleeping bear, or subtly enacted in relation to others, the therapist or the self. A raised eyebrow, a smile of submission, a hesitation about continuing, a telling association, or a tension in the jaw can be guideposts for exploring emotional activation. In addition, repetition of words, phrases or ideas, sequencing, tonal quality and symbolic resonance in the therapeutic exchange can alert us to material that warrants further exploration. As Freud (1905, pp. 77–78) remarked over a hundred years ago, on the futility of keeping secrets,

> He that has eyes to see and ears to hear may convince himself that no mortal can keep a secret. If his lips are silent, he chatters with his fingertips; betrayal oozes out of him at every pore.

We reveal who we are in everything we do. Manifestations of the patient's mental organization can be found in every session because they seep out of every interaction. We listen for the patterns of organization in the many layers of the therapeutic experience. We listen for what is going on between us in the therapeutic encounter. We especially listen for the small manifestations of complex developmental traumas and the defenses developed to deal with them. Being sensitive to these small traces of emotional activation can help therapists grasp the core developmental issues with which their patients struggle.

This kind of listening, listening for the footprints of the past, gives us opportunities to identify unmetabolized, unintegrated patterns of relating that significantly impact patient's lives. In addition, because the intensity of these micro-manifestations is lower, the potential for integration with one's centered sense of self is higher. Working on this level, with the smallest traces of unintegrated childhood experiences provides us with early intervention techniques that enable us to explore defense, enactments and symbolic processes before emotional activation hijacks conscious control. These early interventions are especially valuable when working with patients with trauma histories because with them the potential for destabilizing emotional activation is always lurking just out of sight. Learning how to track the footprints of childhood trauma and activation facilitates engagement during calmer moments when the patient is more receptive to the process. Too much emotional activation will stimulate defenses, dissociative or splitting processes that inhibit integration. Working to help the patient identify, understand and integrate the smaller manifestations of their traumatic childhood experiences without being overwhelmed is a central goal of treatment. Think small, in fact, is a theme that will be repeated many times in many ways throughout this book.

Psychodynamic therapy builds a number of factors into its structure that help us to engage people with and without trauma histories. Primary is the need to create a safe environment. (Herman, 1992; James, 2008; Van der Kolk, 2005, 2013, 2014). Patients will not open themselves up to a stranger without feeling safe.

Helping patients to feel safe enough to tolerate the therapeutic process is one of the challenges of working psychodynamically. Enduring the anxieties of exploring unknown territories and discovering that the enemy is within is a journey not to be taken lightly. It requires courage and a trusted guide to allow oneself to explore this terrain.

We do many things to help patients feel safe but perhaps the most central one is organizing the therapeutic situation as a collaborative one. This mode of relating is important in all therapeutic endeavors, but for those who have abuse and neglect in their histories, it is essential. A collaborative mode of relating immediately addresses the helplessness so many of these patients feel—giving them a voice and a role in the interpersonal process as well as opportunities to have some control of the process through a unique structure of interaction. The structure of the psychotherapeutic situation is discussed extensively in Chapter 3. This structure facilitates the development of integration and observing ego functioning, vital processes involved in recovery from childhood adversity.

We work from a calm and steady state to minimize the risk of emotional hijacking, the reactivation of right brain dominance and its accompanying emotional conviction. We need to be able to listen carefully to the patient, to our own inner voices and to the processes that go on between us. At the beginning of a treatment, we do not know whether a patient has a trauma history, or even when we do, the extent of its impact. This book therefore has a dual purpose: first, to introduce the reader to the fundamental principles of psychodynamic technique; second, to identify and elaborate the way that traces of complex developmental trauma can be used to understand the patient and structure the treatment.

We will begin our journey by examining the building blocks of all psychotherapy. Part I examines the therapeutic foundation, the attitudes and modes of relating that get our adventure off to a good start. Part II briefly outlines the core concepts that are essential in developing a psychodynamic point of view. Generating the skills that enhance our ability to work psychodynamically is addressed in Part III through a section on listening for the layers of how early mental organization is represented in everyday interactions. Finally, although there are as many ways of helping patients as there are patients themselves, the chapters in Part IV are focused on the treatment of complex developmental trauma—helping patients change how they relate to trauma triggering, one of the most important and automatic sequelae of relational trauma. This process involves identifying emotional activation, developing a narrative with the patient that includes an understanding of how the past influences present behavior, and assisting the patient to *actively* engage an inner organization they are necessarily ambivalent about changing.

Exploring the Landscape of the Mind is an overview, a guide to the basic principles of working psychodynamically. Each topic addressed has an extensive history, a history complete with considerable and ongoing debate as to the nature, feasibility or usefulness of many of the topics covered. This primer is presented as one perspective. It is one person's understanding, my own, and so is necessarily limited. My hope is that sharing my path, my process and thinking, giving voice to how I function as a therapist, will provide a starting point for others to think and write about their own work and their own processes. This book is not meant to replace the depth of reading, thinking and development that gifted psychodynamic writers have contributed in over a century of wrestling with the concepts and techniques at the heart of deepening therapeutic engagement. The clinical examples are provided with the generous permission of my patients, many of whom were kind enough to check them for accuracy.

Every professional, teacher, bricklayer, opera singer, sailor or physician, uses certain tools. The psychotherapist is no different. The tools of the trade for psychotherapy are the body, mind, heart and spirit of the therapist. Perhaps more than any other dimension of doing psychotherapy, these tools, carried in the person of the therapist, are critical to successful therapeutic work. Like any set of tools, they need to be developed, practiced and kept in good repair. The Greek proverbs, "know thyself" and "physician, heal thyself," point to a need for self-under-standing and self-assessment as essential aspects of the work. Self-understanding and development come from one's own treatment: an interest in knowing the deepest levels of what is motivating, triggering, exciting and anxiety-producing in a very personal way. This understanding cannot be achieved by reading, coursework or self-analysis alone—we all have blind spots that make understanding incomplete without an analytic collaborator. In addition, doing psychotherapy involves cul-tivating an awareness of intricate aspects of one's own inner life to be able to access transference and countertransference signals. Finally, although aspects of this understanding can be achieved in group settings, fuller exploration in an individual setting is needed for optimum results.

Doing psychotherapy requires an ability to focus on the experience of the self as well as the other. Do not be deceived. Though the therapist does his or her work sitting down, the level of energy required by this kind of focus is considerable. Getting adequate sleep, periods in which one can rest, play, reflect or meditate, as well as adequate time between sessions is part of the routine self-care that optimizes our ability to do our job. We are listening not only to the content of what the patient is saying, but also to how that content is organized by the patient's history, defenses, affects, and memories. And this does not even begin to explore how this content affects the therapist. What kind of symbolic and unconscious meaning does the content carry, how does it stimulate regressive pulls, transference/countertransference enactments, wishes and fears in the therapist as well as the patient? Although we are sitting in one place, doing psychotherapy can be psychologically very taxing. Developing routines of self-care is a necessary aspect of doing the work.

Before beginning any venture, preparing oneself for the nature of the journey is well-advised. Overarching the development of skills that the therapist needs to acquire for this unique collaborative journey are the therapeutic attitudes that powerfully impact the outcome from the very first contact. The following section on attitudes is directed toward developing one's "analyzing instrument" (Isakower, 1957; Grossman, 1992) by exploring those attitudes that have the most impact on maintaining a good therapeutic relationship. These attitudes are dependent upon the therapist's development, temperament and training. Some, we may find, come relatively easily to us. Others will have to be more strenuously cultivated. And some may actively challenge our mettle.

PART I

The Therapeutic Foundation

CHAPTER 1

Therapeutic Attitudes

An attitude has been defined as "a settled way of thinking or feeling about something, a feeling or way of thinking that affects a person's behavior" (Merriam-Webster, 2016). An attitude is a tendency of the mind, an orientation that expresses emotion or intentions. Our attitudes have both conscious and unconscious manifestations and are perceived through the patient's conscious and unconscious experience. The possibility for there being a "good match" between patient and therapist depends on many factors, but among the most important are the implicit attitudes of the therapist.

The attitudes outlined below are essential abilities that create the building blocks for a *personally professional* therapeutic engagement (Adler and Bachant, 1998), a mode of relating to the patient that is at once personal *and* professional. They are not to be considered goals that must be achieved. Acknowledging that we have more or less of some of these abilities is a necessary part of knowing ourselves. We are better off, whatever our strengths and weaknesses, viewing these abilities as ideals that we can strive toward, knowing that they can never be fully realized.

Valuing the Influence of the Past

Valuing the past undergirds all psychodynamic work. An understanding that the past has vital influences on present day wishes, fears, needs, fantasies, thoughts and behaviors is an essential aspect of working dynamically. It is a necessary aspect of understanding that enables the patient to connect with the reasons for maladaptive behaviors. The deeper understanding of self that emerges from an emotionally connected understanding of past experience allows patients in dynamic therapies to maintain their gains better than those in more time limited therapies (Shedler, 2010). The great American novelist, William Faulkner (1951) observed, "The past is never dead. It isn't even past." Therapists do well to keep this in mind.

An understanding of the past is essential because early childhood relationships, losses and attachments structure our conscious and unconscious experience in the present. Linking past and present experience is a vital component of working dynamically and helping patients to know where their wishes, fears and conflicts come from. Especially when patients have experienced complex developmental trauma and can be emotionally ambushed by patterns of relating, thinking and feeling that are beyond conscious control, an appreciation needs to be developed for why these modes of relating have been developed and what keeps patients attached to them. Not grasping the pervasiveness of the way early interpersonal interactions organize present mental functioning leaves therapists tied to the surface content of patients' concerns instead of being able to see the deeper issues with which they struggle.

Respect

The attitude of respect is rooted in an awareness of the separateness that exists between patient and therapist. It involves the humble understanding that only patients can have full access to their inner experience and therefore only patients can decide what is right for them as well as how far to take the therapy. The therapist cannot know the strength and nature of the forces that work for growth or against change. Only the patient has access to their inner dynamics—the fears, fantasies and desires that have not even been articulated. Only the patient can decide how much he or she wants to change. Only the patient can walk in his or her shoes.

Patients who have experienced childhood abuse or neglect often have suffered a lack of respect in their histories. Their wishes have been unheard, their feelings unrecognized, and their behavior controlled so that their survival has depended on constructing a false self or dissociating from their experience of self. Inevitably, these patterns of relating will be reenacted in the therapeutic process. The attitude of respect enables us to listen more carefully to the patient, rather than through the idea that we know what is best. The urgent impulse that we often have to make it better for them is countertransferential. Most importantly, respect gives us the breathing space to be able to sense the presence of a fantasy or enactment so that it can become a focus of the work. Respect embodies patience, the understanding that this work takes time—time for the patient to allow us into the heart of their own darkness, and time to work on changing neural networks to which they are powerfully attached. Expecting that this work should be easy or quick is not respectful.

> Lily came to her session apologizing for being over ten minutes late. It was not the first time. I inquired, "What gets in the way of your being more on time?" Whereas at other times Lily would ward off reflection with a plethora of excuses, this time she replied simply, with a shrug, "It's the same thing every time. I get lost in my thoughts and before I know it, I'm late again." What followed was an exploration of the process of getting lost in her thoughts, including childhood memories of staring out the window for hours on end, imagining that her real family was going to come and rescue her from these crazy, dangerous people she was living with. The multiple determinants of her "getting lost," including her anxieties about our interaction as well as the powerful comfort provided by her dissociation, was then something that we could examine. "Helping" her to pragmatically deal with her lateness (by suggesting that she set an alarm, for example) would have bypassed a significant aspect of relating to herself and others. By attending to the enactment of her lateness with respectful interest and curiosity, we were able to open up a core component of an automatic pattern of relating.

With respect comes the awareness that we cannot "fix" the patient. Respect embodies the conviction that with understanding, the deepest healing will come from within patients themselves. We can help them uncover hidden wishes and fears, confront childhood terrors that inhibit them from leading full lives, and recognize the complexity of their choices. In contrast, telling the patient what to do, by giving advice, for example, can perpetuate patients positioning themselves as children rather than adults, and encourage the enactment of childhood strategies. It can disrupt the process of learning to use their inner selves in directing their own lives. It is not respectful.

Curiosity

Perhaps the most important attitude in the therapist's toolbox is curiosity, the desire to learn more about something. Curiosity helps the therapist to explore the intimate details of an experience knowing that these details are the gateway to the patient's deepest wishes and fears. It has been said of the great painter Vincent Van Gogh that no detail of life was too small or too humble for him (*Loving Vincent*, 2015). Therapists learn to be curious about these details, as well as interested in how things fit together. Openness to the unvarnished experience of the other is the backbone of curiosity. This can be difficult as we all have biases that cloud our ability to accept that the experience of others is necessarily going to be different from our own. A genuine interest in the truest picture of the patient's inner life allows patients to share parts of themselves that may never have been revealed to anyone. Developing the awareness that even tiny details can stimulate associations, thoughts, feelings and fantasies enables both participants to see patterns of organization and excites an interest in understanding.

Therapists also need to be curious about what is *not* being said—what is being left out—and how this is connected to what is being talked about. Being curious beyond the content of what the patient is saying helps the therapist to inquire into the feelings, meaning, and organization of relatedness. It involves learning to ask open-ended questions rather than closed questions or ones that limit the inquiry. Being interested in the details of interactions helps the therapist see and feel where, when, and how the patient is reacting to an inner or outer stimulus. Interpersonally, curiosity has a powerful message for the patient: "I am interested in knowing your genuine self, even if you are bored, angry, upset or despairing." This message, not said in words, but communicated through the action of being curious about the patient's inner life, speaks very loudly. Especially with patients who have relational trauma in their early history, communicating a genuine interest in their experience tells them that the trauma does not put us off, that we want to develop the fullest understanding of who they are.

Non-judgmentalness

Our ability to be curious is undercut if our curiosity is not paired with non-judgmentalness. Patients come to us with problems that involve core emotional issues. Sexuality, aggressive impulses, ability to connect with others, traumas, guilt, shame, childhood wishes and behaviors that are beyond their control are common. Curiosity, a desire to understand where these maladaptive behaviors come from and what maintains them in current day functioning, helps us to move away from judgmentalness. Approaching each person with non-judgmentalness is the next step, essential in order to allow patients to reveal themselves. It is especially relevant for patients with a trauma history, as judgmentalness conveys that the therapeutic situation is not a place of safety. Condemnation of who the patient is (*even if it is silent and not expressed*) compromises the treatment and the possibilities for creating a good working relationship. Trauma often leaves naive and strange ideas fixed in a child's mind. Understanding that no matter how repulsive, frightening, or disturbing we find a patient's experience, there were understandable reasons why the patient developed the way she did helps us to explore rather than to judge.

Empathy

Empathy is our first language. We must be fluent in this language to connect meaningfully with the patient and to further the therapeutic process. Empathy is the ability to understand and emotionally connect with another's feelings, an ability that originally was mediated through early communication in the mother infant dyad. This first language is not the language of words, but that of nonverbal communications. Bodily based emotional expression through voice, tone, eye contact, touching, and gestures is the first language we learn, primal lessons that are expanded with maturation. Infants read these nonverbal communications beneath the words and establish internal working models from what they perceive (Schore, 2015). Therapeutic interactions involve both parties reading between and beneath the words to know and connect with the other as well as themselves. The experience of empathic connection and disconnection stimulates early issues with emotional attunement and, as they are negotiated therapeutically, contribute to the healing process (Abend, 1986; Beres and Arlow, 1974; Kohut, 1977, 1982, 1984; Orange, 1995; Shapiro, 1981; Zwiebel, 2004). Schafer (1959) succinctly described empathy as involving the "inner experience of sharing in and comprehending the momentary psychological state of another person" (p. 345). Empathy provides us with a rich and fertile ground in which the treatment can take root, nourishing the patient's growth. It is an attitude that is essential to dynamic exploration. This is particularly the case with trauma patients who often have histories of empathic misattunement and disordered attachment.

We must distinguish, however, between empathy and over-identification with the patient's experience, where the boundary between patient and therapist blurs. Empathy is not losing oneself in the experience of the patient, but an ability to connect with that experience as a separate self. Boundaries are important. Shared separateness, not merging is the hallmark of a good empathic connection. As therapists, we need to develop the ability to listen with a tension between empathic identification and observing distance (Zwiebel, 2004).

Too much immersion in the process of empathizing deprives the treatment of an outside perspective and the ability to use our therapeutic tools. Especially as we work with patients who have complex developmental trauma in their history (in the beginning of a treatment we do not know the full story), it is important to guard against the danger of over-identification with the patient. We need to connect with the patient's experience, but not so much so that we get locked into it, identified with the very fears and obstacles that paralyze the patient. A fluctuating interplay between empathic resonance and an ability to observe the process is optimal.

Genuineness

Genuineness involves the capacity of the therapist to be who he or she is. Genuineness is based on the ability to accept the wholeness of who we are, a lifelong task whose engagement is essential in the therapeutic interaction. Genuineness involves the capacity to be personally professional. We all know a genuine person when we meet one, but patients who suffered abuse and neglect as children may be more wary in this regard, many having learned that people are not to be trusted. Patients with trauma histories are often watchful that a new person is not a new edition of a former abuser. Attempts to be a better person or a more perfect therapist than one actually is will be sensed and can be read as not being trustworthy. The acceptance of self in all its limitations, on the other hand, is a powerful statement that provides the patient both with a model for self-acceptance as well as the safety of knowing to whom they are relating. It is communicated to patients in many ways, both through the truth of what we say to them as well as through nonverbal expression.

Ability to Accept Limits

Patients have their own agendas, their own timelines, their own limits. As we have ours. Accepting our unique set of limitations as well as the limitations inherent in structuring a course of psychotherapy is a part of knowing ourselves and working in a therapeutic setting. We accept and set limits during every session when we establish a therapeutic frame, are consistently there, are there on time, end the session in a timely way and expect payment when it is due. There are extenuating circumstances— for example, we do not want to escort a sobbing patient out the door. We demonstrate an ability to accept and set limits by maintaining the therapeutic frame and establishing a safe and secure environment in which to work. We also need to be able to accept that we have personal, emotional and intellectual limits. We are humans, not gods, and we all have weaknesses. Being able to accept our own limitations, even as we may be working on them, helps patients to understand that we are *all* limited and that it is not shameful to acknowledge our limitedness or our mistakes. Patients are likely to struggle with limits, often wanting to deny their existence or to test the therapist to see how much he or she can bear. The idea of limits is often packed with powerful, idiosyncratic fantasies that can be fruitfully opened up in the treatment. Using the problems generated by the limits of the therapeutic frame can give us immediate access to core conflicts and issues. Knowing that therapists have boundaries and can accept their own limitedness provides a safety net in which these patients can allow themselves to experience their inner lives.

Another limitation on the therapeutic side is the acknowledgement that we will not be able to work with every patient. We may be triggered by some patients, intimidated by others, or we may find that it is simply a bad match—that we are not able to provide the patient with what he or she needs, in terms of time, financial constraints, or the best psychological match.

It is not our job to make patients accept what we feel they should do. We can help them to do what interests them (as this interest carries their growing edge) and to understand as fully as possible why this is important to them. Therapy is not the treatment of choice for every person at every time. Patience is an integral part of accepting limits. There are no quick fixes in psychotherapy. Patience, especially with the limits and pace of the treatment, is a vital aspect of developing a constructive analytic attitude.

Flexibility

Structure and flexibility are characteristics of all living systems. Flexibility enhances therapeutic effectiveness and enables the therapist to adapt to the needs of their patients. We demonstrate flexibility when we can postpone a question we were going to ask the patient, because we can sense that something in the patient is pressing for expression. Flexibility enables us to follow the patient's flow of associations, rather than being tied to our ideas of what they should be saying, thinking or doing. Flexibility allows us to take in a patient's criticism or anger without becoming defensive. Flexibility enables us to be open to the shifting flow of the patient's associations, giving us the freedom to sail with them into uncharted waters. Especially as we work with patients with traumatic childhood histories, the ability to be flexible will serve us well. We use our flexibility to structure a treatment process that can work for the patient.

Courage

The attribute of courage is essential to the process of psychotherapy. It takes courage to begin and persevere in this voyage into the unknown and to accompany the patient on his or her journey. The therapeutic process is a venture we embark on together, without knowing where it is going to take us. We need to feel safe enough in ourselves to journey into a unique interaction and into the innermost recesses of mental life. We need courage to face and accept the feelings and fantasies that the process will engender in us, the projections through which the patient will see us, and to move toward what patients often want to move away from.

Patients with trauma histories can challenge our courage. What they have to tell us can be shocking, frightening, seductive, embarrassing or disturbing. It takes courage to stay with intense traumatic enactments, ones that often involve the aggressive defenses that patients have evolved to keep themselves safe. It takes courage to listen and to be called out for our mistakes. Our challenge is to use our courage to examine the intensity of the patient's feelings or actions, allowing them to develop their own voice. This enables the patient's experience to be integrated into their sense of self. It takes courage to listen to a traumatized patient, especially if the trauma is being played out in the therapeutic relationship, and to stay with exploring and examining the process instead of merely reacting to it as one would in an ordinary relationship.

Most of all, it takes courage to allow oneself to be used by another in the service of their growth and development. This is perhaps the most difficult aspect of doing psychotherapy: with curiosity and interest, rather than defensive correction, allowing the patient to expand and work through a vision of ourselves that we do not recognize, indeed that we may find deeply disturbing, Allowing ourselves to be the fantasy object to whom the patient is relating is a generous act, one that permits the temporary use of self in the service of developing a better understanding of the other. This suspension, however temporary, of our image of ourselves in the service of another's development challenges us and requires a firmly rooted sense of self.

It takes courage to connect so intimately and emotionally with another, to be known by the other or to be the object of projections that we do not recognize. It takes courage to acknowledge that we are wrong. Like firefighters, we must have courage to move toward the fires from which others run.

Hope

The last attitude in the therapist's toolbox is hope. Hope is a belief based on our knowledge and intimate emotional experience that there is a drive to connect, to bring things together, to grow, and that therapy nourishes this process. Patients with complex histories often come to therapy mired in the helplessness they felt as children when they had few resources to ameliorate their suffering. Their experience of this helplessness often gets

stimulated by and enacted in the therapy, leaving both participants with feelings of hopelessness. Identifying the causes of
the hopelessness as well as the investments that patients have in
maintaining this feeling enable us to help patients change their
relationship with this debilitating feeling. Hope is grounded
in our knowledge that working together to understand our
patients' inner and outer development will enable them to find
new resources, make better decisions and change their relationship with their inner tormentors, what Van der Kolk has spoken
of as "befriending" bodily experience (Van der Kolk, 2014). To
stay with hope through the haze of despair involves being able
to discern the growing edge of the patient's struggles.

There is much more that could be said about each of
these therapeutic attitudes. Instead of talking more about them
abstractly, I will highlight their use as I give clinical examples
throughout the book.

CHAPTER 2

Modes of Relating

One of the first things we learn when we come into the world is *how* we are related to by other people. Are we handled roughly, with loving care, or neglected because of a parent's narcissistic needs? Is the world a safe place or a dangerous one? Whatever the case, how we are related to from earliest infancy will register in our developing minds. How we are related to is our first mode of connecting with others, and although we learn to walk and talk, make music and art and do differential equations, how we relate to self and others is organized during our earliest days and continues to claim an important place in our lives in the present. It is even more consequential in the therapeutic relationship, especially when working with patients who have had traumatic childhood experiences.

There is widespread recognition that the therapeutic relationship is a vital part of the process even though it is essentially left out of manualized therapy approaches and some online talk therapies. Schore (2015) and Ginot (2015) contend that the hallmark of trauma is damage to the relational life and therefore the resolution of trauma must occur in a relational context. *How* the therapist relates to the patient not only makes a difference, often it is the critical factor in the success or failure of a treatment.

By modes of relating I am referring to a quality of relatedness that is consistent and relatively conscious in the mind of the therapist. It involves the mindset with which the therapist communicates. The therapeutic attitudes outlined above contribute to the quality of the therapeutic relationship. But by modes of relating I am referring to the gestalt, the organization of these attitudes and intentions that become a part of our "analyzing instrument." We will go into considerable detail about one of these modes of relating that has been codified as the structure of the therapeutic situation. There are practical and technical reasons why the conventions organizing the therapeutic interaction ensure that therapy facilitates the patient's self-understanding and promotes access to unconscious material. But beyond the structure of the therapeutic situation, which we will address in more detail shortly, modes of relating also have impact on the development and quality of the therapeutic encounter. With patients who have experienced significant adversity or trauma, the first consideration has to be a conscious appreciation of the importance of ensuring safety in the therapeutic relationship.

Ensuring Safety

Our conscious and unconscious attitudes affect the treatment, but in addition, whether we are aware of it or not, we organize the therapeutic situation in ways that profoundly influence the course of treatment. Before we examine the organization of the therapeutic situation in detail, we need to acknowledge the special importance of relating in a context of safety.

Safety and its interpersonal manifestation, trust, is perhaps the most important consideration in working with those who have a history of traumatic childhood experiences (Herman, 1992/1997/2015; Van der Kolk, 2005, 2014). Establishing safety is a precondition for working with this population. Respect for the patient, consistency, genuine and nonjudgmental interest in the patient's experience, and positive regard are qualities of relatedness that help patients feel safe. Structuring safety into the treatment and staying aware of how the therapy process can stimulate fears and fantasies are essential when working with trauma patients. Organizing the therapy around safety is a mode of relating that enables the patient to be more open to those fears, fantasies and feelings that might otherwise derail the treatment.

With those patients who have experienced developmental trauma, what signifies safety may be very different from our own ideas about what safety involves. For some patients, for example, lying on the couch may arouse too much vulnerability to be a useful therapeutic tool. For others, initially avoiding eye contact may be a precondition of being safe. Flexibility comes to our aid here, enabling us to accept a modification of the conditions under which we have to conduct the treatment even as we explore the particular circumstances that led the patient to having these needs at this time. With time, patients reveal what makes them feel safe. Gradually, they learn to tolerate the discomfort that therapy engenders.

We must be aware that creating a safe place for patients can take a very long time. We cannot eradicate fears with appeals to reason. Instead, we can be aware that our mode of relating to patients carries profound meaning and stimulates fantasies of many kinds. If we treat patients as helpless children, not acknowledging their personal agency and assuming that they need us to tell them what to do, they may feel less safe. Patients who have experienced the helplessness of abuse or neglect, for example, need to see *in the treatment process itself* that they can be in control of their own lives. Therefore, efforts to "fix" the problem for the patient are counterproductive and can trigger experiences of helplessness or even assault. The acknowledgement of the patient's personal agency, actualized through a mode of relating that respects their ability to make their own choices, enables patients to feel safer and stronger. Helping patients to reflect on their experience in the safety of nonjudgmental therapeutic interaction engenders safety. Sharing with patients what is noticed or observed without imposing solutions helps patients to connect with themselves and engage the healing process. Ensuring safety is an important mode of relating in work with all patients, but it deserves special attention when working with developmental challenges.

Working Collaboratively

Even how the therapist *thinks* about working with patients will be reflected in the way observations are phrased, questions are asked, and interpretations are made. From the very first encounter, patients are scanning the horizon to pick up salient clues as to how this therapist relates and what unconscious wishes and fears are stimulated by his or her mode of relating. The therapist's relatedness is not only important in what it says to a patient seeking to assess the essence of the person to whom they are considering revealing their darkest secrets and deepest longings. The therapist's mode of relating is also important as a therapeutic factor in and of itself. Actions that we take with our patients are our first language in this relationship, and they speak in very loud voices. Our modes of relating are actions that we employ countless times in any given session. The therapist's relatedness has clinical consequences.

Although it cannot be achieved at all times and in all situations, we strive for a mode of relating that is collaborative. There are times when a patient is so disorganized that a more directive and authoritative approach may be needed, and there are other times when we may need to sit back and give the patient full rein. But generally speaking, relating to the patient collaboratively establishes a balance in which fantasy, transference, enactments, and deeply felt experience can emerge. A collaborative mode of relating can help patients understand how their contribution—through their commitment to free association and sharing with the therapist what comes to mind—is necessary and essential to the therapeutic process. The patient's contribution must be respected and valued. This respect is grounded in therapists' humble acceptance of their role, which is found in helping patients deepen their self-understanding, rather than in directing the therapy. It is, after all, this self-understanding that will give patients better tools with which to navigate their lives.

Problems with establishing a collaborative mode of relating are often connected to countertransferential pressures that therapists put on themselves to know more than they can. These pressures can come from many places, including submitting to the patient's unconscious demands, or ideas inculcated in school that excellence requires knowing everything, to name just two. Mental life is so complex, however, that there are always many things we will not know. Not knowing is not the problem. Not being able to collaborate is. It is a critical problem in therapy because the patient, not the therapist, has the answers. Without this collaboration, the therapist is burdened with trying to accomplish something that is fundamentally beyond his or her reach. In this sense collaboration is essential, for without making the patient our partner and an ally in the treatment, the treatment is severely handicapped.

Collaboration is also important in diagnosing transference-based patterns of relating. Not infrequently, patients come into treatment with expectations that the therapist has the answers to their problems and they turn to the therapist as the authority whom they think they need in order to feel better. The idea that a lack of connection to themselves is part of the problem may be very removed from consideration. Other patients may have grown up in a family in which they felt they had to choose between sadistic dominance or masochistic compliance. To engage in a collaborative relationship could feel disquieting or even downright alien. Safety, for these patients may involve efforts to avoid collaborating, turning instead to familial sado-masochistic patterns of relating. Still other patients have developed fantasies that the only way they can be safe or secure is if they disconnect themselves from their inner lives. Obstacles to establishing a collaborative relationship will give us important information about how patients organize relatedness to self and others.

A collaborative style involves thinking about the relationship as an active partnership. The language we chose and the words we use can convey a collaborative mode of relating. The collaborative therapist often uses the expression "we", as in, "How can we understand this? Or, "we need to better understand your lack of empathy for this needy part of yourself." The idea is that we are in this together. This mode of relating has a much different tone than "You need to better understand your lack of empathy . . . ."—which communicates the idea that the patient is in this alone.

A collaborative style also leaves room for each of the participants. Just as we need to be able to ask patients about their inner experience, we also want to be able to communicate our own. If we have a growing sense that only one person can be in the room, noticing this and inquiring about it is often helpful in revealing attachments and prohibitions that might not otherwise be addressed. For example, a patient may feel impelled to not leave space either for his own reflection or for the therapist to talk because he has childhood expectations that he will be criticized. The early defense of warding off the other by having a lot to say helped him to feel safer. Collaboration is replaced by frantic efforts to control the interaction. Patients who turn immediately to the "expertise" of the therapist have another issue. Frequently, their early history is marked by developing defenses of disconnection from certain vital aspects of self. Connection to self is then replaced by reliance on an external authority. The fantasy here is that the other has the answers that the patient needs. We see this in the expectation that the therapist will be able to tell the patient what to do even on their first meeting. For these patients, collaboration can feel dangerous, while submitting to, or even demanding, the authority of the other generates feelings of safety.

We are demonstrating and communicating collaboration to the patient when we genuinely respect them, aware of the fact that conflicts, defenses, attachments or unconscious fantasies may be getting in the way of their making good choices for themselves. A collaborative mode of relating is communicated to patients in thousands of tiny ways: through our focused engagement, respectful questions, ability to tolerate silence while they reflect on inner experience, creation of an atmosphere that values complexity over dichotomous thinking, etc. Therapeutically, the therapist notices the obstacles to a more collaborative relationship, bringing attention and curiosity to exploring these processes.

Perhaps the most important aspect of a collaborative mode of relating is that it nurtures the development of proactive aspects of self. When the therapist is able to truly appreciate and value that the patient is the only one who can direct his or her own life, the patient is awakened to the idea that experiencing and acting on their own personal agency is not only a possibility, but also a necessity. Maybe for the first time in their lives, patients are able to see themselves as active agents of their own experience.

CHAPTER 3

Structuring the Therapeutic Situation

The process of psychotherapy tests patient and therapist alike, asking both to deal with intense feelings, fears, tensions, losses and acceptance of limitations as well as the inevitably of exposing the self. The framework of the therapeutic interaction provides us with a way to manage the intensity of doing psychotherapy. It gives us a bulwark in the rough waters of transference/countertransference interactions, a beacon in the dark of clinical uncertainty and a bridge that can lead us to the essence of understanding actions. Fundamentally, the frame holds and contains the treatment. We leave it or disregard it at considerable peril.

Robert Langs (1975) gives us a classic definition of the therapeutic frame:

> The ground rules and boundaries of the therapeutic relationship include the following: set fee, hours and length of sessions; the fundamental rule of free association with

communication occurring while the patient is in his chair or on the couch; the absence of physical contact and relative anonymity, physicianly concern, and use of neutral interventions geared primarily toward interpretations; and the exclusive one-to-one relationship with total confidentiality. (Langs, 1975, p. 106)

Langs' definition leaves out the caveat that confidentiality is set aside when the patient is in danger of harming himself or another person. Telling patients about this limit can make them feel safer. Psychotherapy differs from ordinary interactions in that its processes are thoughtfully examined, and its structure has a specific organization. The analysis of interaction is made possible by the development and management of the therapeutic frame, the structure of the therapeutic situation. The frame organizes the treatment just as a question organizes an answer. It helps to keep the therapeutic process on course, through the stresses and seductions of working with the unconscious aspects of countertransference and enactments, interactions that are inevitable in all therapeutic work.

When we work therapeutically, our focus is on maximizing *the emergence of the unconscious* and *the empowerment of the individual*. The therapeutic frame is a mode of relating designed to enhance this dual focus. The frame is an ally of the process, in the sense that it supports this focus. In addition, the therapeutic frame acts to hold the treatment in the face of emotional crosscurrents that can be destabilizing.

In essence, therapeutic frame holds the treatment, contributing to our goal of helping patients to help themselves. Langs (1975) suggests that deviations from the frame are almost always countertransferentially generated.

Every therapeutic interaction has some sort of organizing principles, even if its orienting ideas are not consciously articulated. Ideas, beliefs and goals, even those implicitly held, structure how, when and why we interact with patients. But not every mode of relating furthers the aims of psychodynamic psychotherapy. Some, in fact, can make recognizing unconscious processes more difficult. As an example, a framework that establishes a parent/child interaction, a psychoeducational model or student/teacher structure, does *not* further the goal of maximizing the emergence of unconscious processes or supporting the patient's personal agency. Further, modalities that are based on a call and response, question and answer model, do not leave enough room for inner reflection. This reflection is necessary for associative currents to emerge and for the therapeutic dyad to examine what can initially appear to be unrelated or irrelevant material. Psychodynamic psychotherapy has developed a structure for the therapeutic situation that is designed to maximize our ability to better see unconscious processes and to foster the increasing ability of patients to nurture their own lives. Adler and I (1993) have written extensively about this topic in our paper, "Free Association and Analytic Neutrality: The Structure of the Therapeutic Situation."

Of the therapeutic attitudes that we have discussed, the attitudes of respect, nonjudgmentalness and empathic attunement are essential aspects of generating the "holding" environment that the frame provides for working therapeutically. These attitudes are crucial components of constructing a framework that fosters the emergence of unconscious processes and supports the empowerment of the patient's authentic self.

We can think of these attitudes as holding the therapeutic frame, even as the therapeutic frame holds the treatment. The frame that Adler and I have developed is defined by two extraordinary ways of relating: free association and analytic neutrality. When used together, these modes of relating have a synergistic effect on the therapeutic process.

Each participant has a different job in the analytic process: the patient is tasked with free associating, the therapist with maintaining analytic neutrality. Together, free association and analytic neutrality establish a structure that provides boundaries, destabilizes neurotic equilibrium, and enables us to explore motivation in depth. The therapeutic process activates powerful emotional triggers in both participants, and therefore requires a structure that can absorb and contain these forces. The frame is the most essential aspect of managing the intensities of the analytic encounter, intensities that are fueled by the activation of fantasy, transference, countertransference and enactment. Free association and analytic neutrality provide the therapeutic situation with stability in the wake of intense emotional currents. The therapeutic frame is a "carefully structured situation in which a spontaneously unstructured relationship can safely and meaningfully unfold" (Adler and Bachant, 1998, p. 35). It is the foundation of the therapeutic process, holding patient and therapist alike within a contained field that channels and absorbs the intensities of relating in depth.

Free Association

Adler and I understand free association as a truly radical proposition focused on the patient's freedom of expression. This is not an easy assignment for the patient, as revealing oneself to another without regard for normal social conventions can be a daunting task. Free association asks even more: it asks patients to verbalize what comes to mind without evasion or self-censorship, even if it involves thoughts, feelings and fantasies about the therapist. In psychodynamic psychotherapy, the therapist is granted privileged access to the patient's inner life, with the understanding that ordinary considerations of privacy will be set aside. Most people have never done this before coming into treatment. It is helpful therefore to let patients know at the beginning of the treatment that psychotherapy is a *collaboration* in which the patient's communicating everything that comes to mind is an essential part of the therapeutic process. We explicitly ask the patient to tell us what comes to mind, even if it is disturbing, embarrassing, confusing, sexual, shameful, aggressive, outlandish, etc. Mentioning the importance and value of sharing such thoughts as they arise about the therapist often furthers the work as well as patients' understanding of the process and the significance of their own contribution.

Many therapies are based on the patient's *conscious* awareness of their experience. Psychodynamic psychotherapy, on the other hand, is organized around gaining access to fantasies, fears, wishes, and the powerful, emotionally driven representations of *unconscious* processing. Free association gives the patient room to reflect, and to value the associations that emerge in the interaction. As the patient reports what comes to mind, issues on the edge of consciousness that have been warded off because of their painful nature are brought to the center of therapeutic attention. Free association develops a structure in which the patient gains access to deep levels of intrapsychic processing in the context of an interpersonal interaction. Analytic focus alternates between a focus on the patient's inner world and a focus on the interpersonal relatedness with the therapist and others. Pine (1993) describes this shared experience as a powerful therapeutic factor that is inherent in the structure of the therapeutic situation itself.

Free association symbolically represents many aspects of relatedness: linkage to the body and bodily sensations; early mother-child intimacy characterized by uncontrolled exposure, unconditional acceptance and separation issues, to highlight just a few. Free association is designed to evoke the most vulnerable aspects of self—the fantasies, wishes, fears, and conflicts that have been warded off. A most useful aspect of working with free association is that its derailment, when it can be identified, offers patient and therapist a marker for the emergence of defense, providing the patient/therapist dyad with a map of the patient's resistances as they are mobilized in the context of the relationship. Free association helps patient and therapist to negotiate resistance and provides access to the dynamic unconscious. It also structures an asymmetrical intimacy into the therapeutic situation that enables the patient to progressively trust exposing deeper levels of experience. But it serves another very important function: It organizes the treatment situation around an ongoing confrontation with compulsive self-judging and self-punishing tendencies. Through the continual action of struggling to say what comes to mind without censorship, the patient is quietly but consistently working through aspects of self-inhibitory functioning. All this is made possible by the enhanced opportunity to become an observer as well as a participant in one's own internal process. This process differs significantly from solitary introspection and more interactive modes of relating. Free association allows patients to view themselves as an *object* of the process, as well as an *active contributor* to and an *ally* of the treatment. This active process enhances the development of observing, collaborative and integrative ego functions.

Analytic Neutrality

Neutrality has a special meaning in psychodynamic thinking. It does not refer to hiding one's personality or feelings. It does *not* mean that the therapist is emotionally neutral or unexpressive. It does *not* mean that the therapist should not reveal who he or she is, for that is not possible. We communicate who we are in thousands of actions with our patients all the time—through our tone of voice, facial expressions, dress, voice messages, therapy offices, etc. We cannot hide who we are. Analytic neutrality is a technical concept in the therapeutic situation. It has an important purpose: *to create a setting in which the patient's associations and unconscious processes can emerge.* The technical mode of neutrality developed to help the therapeutic *partnership gain easier access to the feelings, fantasies, conflicts and projections that we want to see more clearly.* Adler and I speak of technical neutrality as involving three dimensions: neutrality in relation to conflict, neutrality in relation to sequence and neutrality in relation to transference.

Neutrality in Relation to Conflict

The neutral therapist acknowledges what is true *in the patient's experience*—the patient's wishes, fears, feelings, fantasies, beliefs and intentions are accepted for what they are *with the understanding that they are to be explored, for there is always more.* The therapist makes no demand that the patient's experience should be different from what it is. The neutral therapist does not tell students who don't want to go to classes that they should go. Nor does the neutral therapist tell the wife who wants to leave her husband that she should try to work on the marriage, nor the son who feels guilty about his father's death that he should not feel guilty. Neutrality asks the therapist to acknowledge the truth of the patient's psychic reality, but also to understand that the patient's reality is complex and multifaceted. Conflict is always present. What is passionately felt one day can give way the next to a very different experience, as other dimensions of the patient's experience come to the fore. It can be difficult to find a way to acknowledge the patient's subjective reality without using the authority of the analysis to validate a biased or one-sided perspective. For example, patients may demand that we agree with them that their father didn't love them, but to do so would be to deny "the more"—the ways in which the father did love them—despite abuse, neglect or criticism. Neutrality in relation to conflict asks the therapist to be a patient listener, mandating a reserve in responsiveness that leaves room for "the more." Because all relationships are ambivalent, and because many patients begin therapy thinking in black and white, leaving room for "the more" in our responses avoids premature closure and limiting understanding.

Neutrality in Relation to Sequence

Neutrality in relation to sequence refers to the importance of respecting the patient's unique path in the therapeutic process. The neutral therapist understands that the patient's process is determined by *multiple* factors and accepts the importance of the sequence in which issues, associations and concerns are brought forward. For example, patients often speak about the parent with whom they are the least conflicted first. Being able to talk about the relationship with the more conflicted parent often requires the safety of a more grounded therapeutic relationship. Respecting the ordering of the patient's sequence gives us optimal access to the patient's process. We practice technical neutrality when we wait to see how the patient will start the session, for example, for to do otherwise is to obscure seeing the context of where the patient is coming from. Mental processing is extraordinarily complex. In addition to the issue of clouding the patient's latent content, we must have the humility to recognize that only the patient will be able to direct us to his or her unconscious wishes and fears. The neutral therapist does not try to dictate the sequence or timing of issues, but instead, respects the patient's process.

Neutrality in Relation to Transference

The most demanding aspect of analytic neutrality is neutrality in relation to the patient's transference. At some point, inevitably, patients see us primarily through the eyes of their relationships with their primary caretakers. Whether we become the patient's critical superego, the hovering mother, the gratifying grandparent, the abusive father or any of an infinite number of characters in patients' relational dramas and fantasies, there will be times when our patients will experience us very differently from the way we experience ourselves. It is, perhaps, the most difficult dimension of therapeutic work to allow ourselves to be used as a transference object in ways that are alien to our own self experience. Yet, it is through the acceptance, engagement and exploration of these transference projections that we have the most extensive opportunity to help our patients grow. Maintaining neutrality in relation to the transference, allowing the patient's transference projections to develop in the therapeutic relationship, brings emotional conviction to the process. The focus of the treatment moves beyond the content of the patient's experience into the process of what is going on in the treatment room. Working with these transference projections by being curious about them, examining the feelings, fears and fantasies connected with them in the here and now relationship with the therapist has an immediacy that is not matched by simply talking *about* something from a distance. Added is the component of felt, emotionally connected experience. Using transference interpretations framed in relation to the therapist to organize the patient's unformed, often archaic impulses, feelings, conflicts and anxieties defuses pressures within the dyad and permits the mapping of uncharted territory.

We must not forget that in addition to having transference activity in relation to the therapist, patients will also relate to the structure of the therapeutic *situation* with transference projections. How the treatment is organized will stimulate transference fantasies, wishes and fears—the nature of the boundaries communicated by the therapist, how the room is furnished, how the therapist dresses, how the fees are collected, and so on. These transferences to the frame are opportunities to elicit exploration about patients' expectations and how they organize their world. They are to be welcomed as occasions to inquire about the important aspects of the patient's experience rather than as rules that must be followed.

Neutrality in relation to the transference suggests that we conscientiously strive to avoid any attitude, posture, or technique that consistently predisposes patients to develop a particular kind of transference experience, either through undue frustration, gratification, support, persuasion, or moral pressure (Adler and Bachant, 1998, p. 49). The challenge is to be conscious of directing or controlling the patient's transference, to have them like us for instance, or to suggest that they be the good patient for us. Instead, our goal is to be open to acknowledging, exploring and being curious about the transference activity that does develop. This is easier said than done, as part of the psychodynamic process involves being continually drawn into enacting rather than analyzing patient's transference processes. These projections and enactments, along with the fantasies, wishes and fears they carry, can be an enriching part of the process, *if they can be recognized, explored and brought into the treatment.* This oscillation between being able to listen to the patient as an observer and being caught up in participating in the patient's transference activity is an essential current in the flow of developing understanding. Without it, we do not gain the deepest understanding of the patient's experience. Neutrality involves striving not to direct or control the patient's transference but rather a commitment to exploring it.

When we organize the structure of the psychodynamic situation around free association and analytic neutrality, we are providing a framework that holds the treatment through the stresses and storms of analytic work. This framework is organized to maximize the emergence of the patient's latent feelings, fantasies and conflicts. It also provides numerous benefits that are intrinsic to this structure. Doing psychotherapy is an intense process that continually tests its participants. Adopting a structure that contains and holds the treatment helps us to manage its intensity and keep the process on course.

PART II

Core Concepts in Psychodynamic Work

"There is a prophet within us, forever whispering that behind the seen lies the immeasurable unseen."
— Frederick Douglass

A framework that can hold the process through the currents of a treatment is the mast that holds our vessel to its course, but in order to chart our direction we need to identify a few essential features of the territory we will explore. We will begin by looking at fantasy, because fantasy helps us to navigate the dark skies of the mind. Fantasy gives us access to how mental life is organized. We will explore the intimate relationship between trauma, fantasy and transference, examine the emotional connection brought through transference/countertransference activity, and end our journey by exploring resistance and the principle of multiple functioning. Treatment of these concepts is limited in scope to my own perspective and necessarily omits substantial work in the field. This book is a primer, focused on what is essential in a practical understanding of beginning psychodynamic treatment. Further exploration of these concepts is essential.

CHAPTER 4

Fantasy

We turn first to fantasy because fantasy is the window to our soul, to the hopes, dreads and desires that make us uniquely who we are. Fantasy reveals the patient's underlying mental structure, giving us a glimpse of how the past has been experienced and adapted to. Fantasy shows us how the mind is organized. Understanding the patient's mental organization grounds our listening and our interventions.

The concept of fantasy in psychodynamic work casts a much broader net than common usage suggests. Psychodynamically, the process of fantasy-making translates into narrative form the wishes, fears, defenses, ideas and modes of relating that organize experience (Isaacs, 1948; Solms, 1996). Our histories of love and abuse, our defenses against pain, our attachments to others, our trauma, automatic patterns and moral imperatives are blended together in the images, expectations and narratives we create in fantasy. The process of fantasizing gathers the many threads of our mental life and weaves them into a tapestry through which we can apprehend our inner world. Attending to fantasy allows us to see the colors, flow and patterns of the patient's mental organization. *Fantasy allows us to access and represent inner experience*, synthesizing an infinite number of mental processes that are beyond conscious apprehension. Fantasy represents these processes to us in a form that speaks the language of our experience.

Fantasy has a double meaning in therapeutic work. In popular usage, people recognize that they have particular fantasies, for example, of hooking up with an attractive potential partner or anticipating how painful their next dental appointment will be. This way of thinking about fantasy refers to the *content* of specific dreams, wishes and fears that are grounded in our emotional history and experience. These fantasies can be either conscious or unconscious. Many people have written about this aspect of fantasy (Arlow, 1969; Beres and Arlow, 1974; Brenner, 1982; Goodman, 2015; Ellman and Goodman, 2017; Levin, 1996; Smith, 1977). Brenner (1982) speaks of this aspect of fantasy as a compromise between different aspects of mental functioning: inner impulses, defenses against them and moral considerations that coalesce into the familiar narratives that spur creative growth or keep us safe.

This meaning of fantasy is concerned with the *content* of the particular fantasy. Implicit in this content understanding of fantasy is an appreciation of the fact that fantasies always have an emotional, evaluative dimension. To oversimplify, our fantasies carry core emotional experience including wishes, fears, early defenses and moral imperatives. They are focused on moving toward pleasure or away from the anticipation of pain. Like consciousness itself, which always an has intrinsically evaluative dimension, fantasy "tells us how we feel about things" (Solms and Turnbull, 2002, p. 105).

While all fantasies have a specific content, in a developmental sense, the content of fantasies grows up with us, coalescing into basic themes and changing over time with maturation and experience. Fantasies serve multiple functions in our psychic economies: they gratify wishes, warn us of danger, protect us from inner fears, defend us from painful memories, spur us to action, give voice to creative urges and sustain us in times of trouble. Fantasy enhances our experience of being in the world. We could even say that fantasy makes our bodily experience of the world intelligible.

But there is another dimension of fantasy that may be even more important. The *process* of fantasizing is a manifestation of the organizing functions of the mind. We look for fantasy not only to access the *content* active in a patient's inner life, but also to allow us to see into the *process* of how that inner world is being organized, *how* the person is synthesizing the buzzing, blooming confusion of life. In this sense, fantasy refers to an integrative function of mind that carries and manifests brain processes that cannot be represented in other ways. Fantasy is an aspect of reflecting on the self, a type of consciousness that is mediated through words and self-talk. (Solms, 1996). Fantasy brings together various aspects of mental functioning into a coherent narrative that captures and symbolizes significant, emotionally grounded themes in the patient's experience. Describing fantasy as an aspect of the integrative functioning of mind alerts us to an understanding of fantasy that is importantly based in *process*, as well as content.

The *process* of fantasizing represents our inner mental organization, one that is active and present all the time. Arlow emphasizes that "fantasy activity, conscious or unconscious, is a constant feature of mental life" (Arlow, 1969, p. 5). Susan Isaacs captures this dual essence from an object relations perspective when she describes fantasies as "the mental corollary, the psychic representative of instinct" present therefore in all experience (Isaacs, 1948, p. 81). *Fantasy is a representation of the organizing dimension of mental activity, one that carries the emotionally based, inner narrative of our history.* In this sense, fantasies and the process of fantasy-making are with us all the time, from the beginning of life—before we could walk or talk or smile.

Most of us have heard the expression, "cells that fire together wire together." Generally, we understand this to mean that repetitive experiences become organized in the brain into neural networks that are more easily triggered than those which are less activated. They become well-oiled, what we call potentiated, so that they are more likely to be activated again. Repeated use of neural networks engenders more probability that these networks will be stimulated. And just like muscles that are not used will atrophy, not exercising certain neural networks also results in less probability that these networks will fire. Thinking about these mind/brain realities on a psychological level enables us to understand another level of why our patients repeat maladaptive behaviors in their relations with others even when these behaviors do not make the situation better. Our brains are primed to react quickly and automatically to situations that stimulate early modes of relating, memories, and fantasies that carry deep seated emotional wishes, fears and defenses. Especially when dealing with childhood relational trauma, early experiences and expectations become automatically wired into our mental functioning. Traces of these early unintegrated experiences have a readiness to be activated by the fantasies stimulated by current interpersonal realities.

Jerry and Abby came to couple's treatment because they found they couldn't control their bickering. They were getting angry at each other all the time, and even though they still loved each other, they were growing increasingly doubtful that they could go on. Jerry was especially triggered by Abby's obliviousness to how her words or actions would affect him. Abby felt endangered by her husband's explosiveness, and would typically withdraw into a sullen silence, punctuated by passive aggressive remarks that would enrage him even more. Intimacy often stimulates the emergence of patterns of relating that were wired together early on—after all, these patterns of relating were formed in the crucible of our earliest relationships. Jerry and Abby needed to find a way to stand outside the patterns that automatically stimulated early experience (for Jerry a lack of connection to his emotional core that characterized his relatedness to his father; for Abby, a readiness to see in her husband the remnants of an angry and tumultuous relationship with her mother). Working on their relationship involved first understanding that they were triggering each other and then developing an ability to identify the precursors of emotional activation. They also both needed to learn to take more responsibility for their own happiness, rather than expecting or demanding that the other should give it to them, fantasies that were deeply rooted in childhood longings to be well taken care of by their parents. Only after this initial work could they move on to being able to accept their reactiveness while still working on its automaticity. The final stage of their treatment involved developing a reflective space between the impulse to be triggered and the present-day interaction. This took time and active engagement with themselves and each other. Abby's fantasy that intimate relations are not safe and Jerry's fantasy that he could only relate through exploding or cutting off were being automatically and powerfully triggered by their interpersonal life together. These modes of relating had been operative from such an early age that they were enacted seamlessly in present day experience with each other. Their fantasies carried a neural mental set through which they perceived and related to the other.

Collectively, fantasies are an enduring, intrinsic, emotionally based aspect of mental functioning. Important thoughts, expectations, wishes and fears prime our neural networks, increasing a tendency to engage through a certain mental set. Through emotionally based self-understanding, whether conscious or unconscious, fantasies connect body and mind. They represent subjective, inner experience, enabling complex mental processes to be experienced consciously. By uncovering, examining and exploring fantasies we help patients to understand a deeper level of their inner organization.

This experience-near way of talking with the patient through fantasy enables the patient to immediately identify with what the therapist is saying and vice-versa. Looking at the things that go on inside us from the same point of view as our patients allows the unconscious to come to life (Solms, p. 112). Solms contends that the greatest virtue of the concept of unconscious fantasy is "it lays bare the causes of our patients' suffering in a language that patients themselves can identify with, and it thereby renders the unthinkable thinkable" (Solms, 1996, p. 115).

As soon as Edith sat down, she told me that the dinner party she had previously spoken with me about was this weekend and that she was dreading it. "I'm hosting it," she said, "and I don't want to go!" She smiled a little, but there were tears in her eyes. "I'm just dreading it!"

she reiterated. *I took note of the repetition of the word dread, which told me that connection to her feeling state was intense. What was setting off this intense feeling? Could this feeling be a trace of childhood feelings and fantasies? What was getting activated that generated such intensity?* Edith elaborated that she had invited her best friends and another couple whom she and her husband had gotten to know and like, but that her intense feeling of wanting to call the dinner off was almost unbearable.

I returned to her feeling with a general invitation to explore the experience of dread: "Sounds like we really need to understand this experience of dread."

I don't know . . . . It's too much responsibility, too much pressure: I have to be a good cook, have a great house, make everyone feel good, make sure everyone is happy. It's too much. I just don't want to do it.

"Sounds awful," I replied. But what is it that you don't want to do: the dinner party or putting these oppressive demands on yourself?

Edith thought about this for a moment. "I see what you are getting at. I don't want to put these demands on myself but it's just the way I'm built. When I'm with other people, I have to be the pleaser, I have to make everything right. I have to give up myself to take care of everyone else. The only time I can be myself is when I'm alone."

I thought about how what Edith was saying applies to our relationship in the transference. About how she might feel a need to please me or to get away from me in our interactions. And there had been occasions in the past where Edith cancelled her session for various reasons. At this moment, however, I felt that staying with her pressing concern was most needed. Edith needed a deeper understanding of the pattern she was becoming aware of. I responded, "No wonder you hate being with other people. You don't give yourself permission to be yourself with others and you put oppressive demands on yourself to boot . . . Has it always been this way?"

is this
pmy Dirt

"It was always this way with my mother and my father! "she exclaimed. I had to play music with my father to keep him happy, and I definitely had to give myself up with my mother in order to be in her good graces. I knew that if I wasn't doing what she wanted me to do I didn't have a chance. She never liked me. I learned very early on that the only time I could be myself was when I was alone in my room doing my art projects."

"So it's not really that you hate being with other people, but that you hate the way you disconnect from yourself and become a people pleaser."

Edith was operating in her present-day life with expectations that belonged to her family of origin. The core fantasy that if she did not disconnect from herself, she would not be loved was driving her relations with friends as well as how she related to herself. The primary issue was not whether or not she hosted her dinner party, but whether she had to give herself up to be with other people. Edith developed this idea from her early relations with family members, especially from her childhood idea that her mother did not love her and oedipally infused fantasies about her father.

Fantasy is a core mental process that helps us to see and understand a primary organizational/synthetic aspect of mental activity. Other mental functions, however, also influence the structuring of mental life. Core attachments and unconscious conflicts, which we see in the processes of resistance and defense, are inevitably stimulated by childhood anxieties. Learning to identify core unconscious conflicts helps patient and therapist alike to understand feelings and actions that otherwise remain inaccessible. Conflict, especially infantile conflict, is a central, inescapable aspect of mental functioning, structured into how our minds are organized. In a similar way, the compromising, integrative functioning of the mind is operative all the time, synthesizing wishes, fears, moral messages, defense and feelings. Fantasy-making uses attachments and core unconscious conflicts with the omnipresent process of synthesizing to create the compromise formations that give form and structure to the individual's experience. Lynch (2018) contends that it is the ever-present hidden structure of these compromise formations that allows fantasy to organize drive, defense, moral imperatives and punishments through an endless series of oscillating transformations to represent inner experience.

CHAPTER 5

The Intimate Relationship between Fantasy, Transference and Emotional Activation

We cannot think about trauma without understanding how the patient is fantasizing about the triggering childhood experience.

As we consider the relationship between trauma and fantasy, it is important to remember that the mind is always constructing its reality. The mind (how we think and feel about our inner and outer world) is not static. It is active, always in process, endlessly constructing meaning, conflict, defense, strategies for safety, gratification, moral concerns etc. This process of constructing reality is ever present. We must remember, however, that the flexibility of psychological construction is balanced by a framework of mental organization that remains relatively stable (Adler and Bachant, 1998). When dealing with complex developmental trauma, we need to be thinking about how and why the patient is constructing the trauma in this way at this

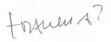

time, as well as developing an understanding of the *framework* in which this constructing is taking place. With development and maturation, dominant themes emerge from cumulative attachments, conflicts and trauma that stay relatively constant in each person's experience.

These themes are given life through fantasy.

As a representation of how the mind organizes and makes meaning of past and present engagement, fantasy infuses the patient's experience at all times, including during treatment. Fantasy, anchored in a synthesis of inner and outer realities, is the ground spring of transference. Transference is valued for its ability to crystallize the meaning of current patterns of inter-action as well as its capacity to uncover the perpetually active unconscious wishes and fears from childhood that continue to organize experience (Bachant and Adler, 1997). The therapy relationship stimulates preformed transference wishes and fears even as it assesses, constructs and organizes relatedness in the present.

Transference dynamics infuse our entire being because as a subset of fantasy, transference mediates unconscious organization. Even realistic and appropriate responses have transference aspects. Like fantasy, transference is a ubiquitous process—transference activity can carry representations of a person, a place, a mental structure or even a process, such as a mode of relating. Hanna Segal (1957), for example, in her paper, *Fear of Death*, spoke about the transference of a cold and unloving mother that was projected onto the country a patient lived in—the patient spoke of how the cold climate was going to kill him. A patient of mine who had been born with whoop-ing cough and whose mother's devoted care had "saved her life" developed a mode of victimizing herself to continually call out for the mother of her infancy. This patient jokingly said that for a while, she could feel "victimized by a red light!" How this patient felt victimized by me was an important part of our work together, and was expressed in her reaction to my boundaries, her requests for special treatment, (a few extra minutes, a glass of water, more or less air conditioning, a delay in payment, etc.) and fantasies she had about my involvement with other patients. Another patient enacted with me her childhood experience of being more trouble than she was worth by continually cancelling and changing her session time. Transference activity infuses enactments and captures the continuing influence of organizing principles and imagery from the patient's formative years (Adler and Bachant, 1998; Stolorow and Lachmann, 1994/1995). White (1996) speaks of transference/resistance as a bridge from the intrapsychic world of the patient to the interpersonal world of the analytic situation. Adler and Bachant (1998) describe transference as both a derivative of unconscious fantasy and an integrator of subjective experience. Transference activity enables us to actualize our unique amalgam of inner and outer experience in a form we can all recognize.

Trauma and fantasy have been connected from the beginning of psychoanalysis. Freud (1905) recognized early on that trauma is inevitably, inescapably linked to fantasy, to how the person perceives and organizes the traumatic event. Understanding the relationship between trauma and fantasy reminds us that there is no one-to-one correspondence between trauma and resultant symptoms. There is no simple cause and effect paradigm. Instead, multiple factors converge to determine how trauma is organized and layered into the individual's mind at each stage of development. External factors are often involved in complex developmental trauma, but most importantly in psychotherapy, trauma is an inner process. *Trauma is organized intrapsychically.* The meaning that the individual ascribes to the childhood experience is determined in large part by that person's inner-life. Fantasy—a synthesis of biological realities, expectations, early wishes, fears, thoughts and relational enactments—shapes how trauma is perceived, organized and integrated into the individual's identity, character and psychology, in short, into every aspect of personality.

Fantasy is crucial in another way as well. As a representation of how brain/mind processes work, fantasy activity gives us the bones of transference/countertransference phenomena. Brain driven expectations and assumptions that develop in interaction with significant others are organized into narratives that are not always conscious but are represented in fantasy. This organization has at its center the emotional connectedness that was developed through these early interactions (Panksepp, 1998; Schore, 2015; Ginot, 2015). In this way, fantasy, mediated through transference, plays a central role in determining our conscious and unconscious choices.

Therapeutically, we "see" and experience the patient's mental organization through the core transference configurations that are brought into the treatment room. Transference brings both the content and process aspects of fantasy into meaningful representations of fundamental issues and conflicts.

Lily started talking about a problem she had been having at her workplace. She works as an executive assistant for a very exacting attorney in a large law office. The issue involved two calls that had inadvertently been omitted from the team calendar. The error terrified Lily and she spent considerable time obsessing about it, trying to find a way to deal with it. She had a consuming feeling that she had to both find a way to hide her transgression from her boss, as well as a compelling impulse to confess her wrongdoing. In reality, the fact that these two calls were not on the calendar was not even Lily's responsibility as it was the job of another assistant to take care of this. Moreover, the calls were weeks away and the calendar was updated daily so there was ample opportunity to fix the problem. When she approached the assistant, who was responsible for the calendar, Lily was astounded that the assistant simply, and without any evidence of anxiety, put the items onto the manager's calendar. "I was dumbfounded," she remarked.

"You expected the other assistant to react to the situation with the same anxious anticipation that you had," I replied. "I did, she said. "I couldn't believe it wasn't a big problem for her." *"You expected your boss to explode like your father did when you were a child, and you imagined your co-worker would feel the same dread that you felt when you were in his presence."* "It was truly eye-opening for me to see how lightly she took the problem," she said.

Lily then talked about the email she sent to me saying that she would be out of town and asking if we could do our session by phone. "I was so surprised, she commented, "at what a nice and kind email you sent me back. I thought you would be mad at me." *"Why would I be mad at you?" I replied, interested in evoking her fantasy.* "I don't' know, I guess I always think I've done something wrong, that I'm going to get in trouble if I ask for something, anything, but especially something that I want." I took note of the way her transference expectation of my reaction paralleled in sequence and structure the expectations she had of how much trouble she'd get in if her boss discovered her mistake with the items on the calendar, and ultimately how angry her father would become if she was any trouble at all. Soon after this exchange Lily recounted an episode in which she was sitting at breakfast with her mother and her father where her mother was making cheese sandwiches for the children's lunch boxes. Lily's mother exclaimed, "Oh, I forgot! You don't like cheese sandwiches!" Lily was terrified to admit this in front of her father who she knew would explode at a request for special treatment. "Oh, I like them now. I really like them," she told her mother, beginning a pattern of denial of what she liked and wanted that lasted for years.

If we learn how to listen for fantasy and its transference manifestations, we can see indicators of mental organizing in every session. This is especially important when working with complex developmental trauma. Trauma is designed by evolution to be remembered in order to prepare us for the world in which we live. It is activated by similarities of many varieties (sensory perceptions, structural similarities, temporal associations, etc.) depending of the strength of the original trauma. It is always in the room. This perspective gives us endless opportunities to access primary organizing factors of our patient's traumatic and conflictual experience. Significantly, it allows us to work with the patient at a moment when ego functions have not been overwhelmed by more intense emotional activation. Working with the smallest manifestations presented to us through the medium of the patient's fantasy enables us to access, in the immediacy of the present, the heart of our patient's suffering.

Vita started her session by describing how, compared to many of the members of her job-hunting class, her job-hunting statistics (how many emails she sent, how many phone calls she made, how many interviews she went on) were consistently at the bottom of her group. She spoke about how she woke up in the middle of the last night with overwhelming feelings of dread and asked her husband if she could cuddle with him as she thought that touching him would help ease her anxiety. It did. *I wondered if this tentative reaching out to her husband was an enactment of her looking for the lost mother of her early childhood, a topic that had been a central focus of our work for some time.*

Vita asked the question, "Why would I have such intense feelings of dread?" *I saw that Vita was reflecting on her experience, allowing herself to observe it from a place other than being totally caught up in it. Wanting to support her newly emerging ability, I commented that I thought this was a very important question.* Vita replied that she didn't understand it because even while the reality was painful, it was not filled with dread. She gave an example of how she reached out to ask for a ten-minute chat with a person she had met and liked years ago and the response she had gotten from him was: "Tell me why I would want to talk with you for ten minutes?" As off-putting as that response had been, Vita didn't allow it to put her off. She wrote back that when she had met him years ago, she had liked him a lot and communicated that she was now exploring the job market. He immediately softened, told her that he was now in India and to call him next week. Vita used this example to highlight the fact that even when things were difficult in her job search, she managed to make something work. The reality was not commensurate with her feeling of dread. Vita remarked that she could see that her feelings were out of proportion to what was happening in the real world. Going back to her overwhelming feeling of dread on the job search, Vita said, "I feel like I am looking for something . . . but I don't even know if it is there." *This was a phrase that struck a chord in me. It shone with significance. In my mind's eye, I saw Vita as a little girl, a toddler (whose world had been forever changed by the births of three additional children in close succession), looking for the kind of contact with her mother that she had become accustomed to, and doubting that she would find it ever again. I mused to myself that she often connected the experience of not finding her mother with thinking that the loss was her fault.* I told Vita that I was struck by her phrase and asked her to let herself fully take in the experience of "looking for something and not even knowing if it was there." What does this bring to mind? *I repeated her phrase so that she could hear it from another's voice.*

Vita became teary and spoke first of her job hunt—the "humiliation" of not being wanted and having to try so hard to get what she was looking for. The experience of humiliation was being triggered here. Clearly, Vita did not relate to her job search as a hunt for treasure that was out there and could be found with diligent effort. For her, the process of looking for a job had taken on a very different emotional meaning. It had become imbued with the "humiliating" emotional experience of trying, often in vain, to reconnect with a loving mother who had been lost to the many caretaking responsibilities of having four children in a row. Vita's experience of her job hunt was an enactment of her earliest traumatic memories of looking for the mother she had had and doubting that she would find her.

We must remember that traumatic fantasies can be re-enacted not only in interpersonal relationships, but also in how the patient relates to herself and her world. Here Vita re-enacted her search for her lost mother in her search for a job, a search she felt consequently hopeless about. I commented that her feelings about her job hunt sounded eerily similar to her experience of looking for the mother she lost when she was such a young child. Vita understood immediately what I referred to and spoke about how not being able to remember the experience made it difficult to believe that this had happened. I responded that we remember in different ways, recalling in my mind's eye Bessel Van der Kolk's (2014) admonition that "the body keeps the score." Although she didn't have a conscious memory of looking for her mother and not knowing if she would be there, she was remembering the experience *in her body, in her actions.* After talking about this possibility, Vita told me something that she had never mentioned before. She said that during the time when she was very little, her father would frequently be away on fishing trips for very long periods of time, sometimes for as long as a week, so that only one parent was available to the children at a time when Vita was desperately trying to connect.

The grip of Vita's debilitating fantasy and automatic defensive responses is very strong. Vita and I have talked about the effect of her early family experience from many perspectives, and Vita's developing understanding has helped her in her struggle against feelings and impulses stemming from early emotional losses. Vita is still vulnerable, however, to finding herself automatically switching into right brain dominated emotional conviction that brings up feelings of despair and hopelessness related to searching for the connectedness she lost so early. Note that I am not describing Vita as having an abusive or neglectful mother. In fact, it is clear that Vita's mother loved her. What we are seeing are the consequences of the unconscious fantasy narrative that Vita herself developed, one that sustained a powerful grip on her thinking, feeling and behavior. The emotionally activating association in this instance was the job hunt which embodied the "humiliating" experience of trying so hard with so little hope to get what she wanted.

The tools that help us to explore effects on the continuum of early childhood adversity require us to reevaluate our understanding of trauma. An appreciation of the role of fantasy in how the destabilizing childhood event is perceived is essential here. A significant degree of treatment for complex developmental trauma is focused on trauma as event—something that happened *to* the patient, something they were forced to endure. But a focus on the person as the *object* of the trauma, and a focus on trauma as a *discrete event* obscures a *process* understanding of trauma, as well as a vision of the person as *active agent*. Trauma is not only an event that happens *to* people. It is, in addition, a *process living within the person* that generates mental and physical organization. People organize the adversity they experience actively, though not always consciously, in ways that are mediated by emotionally based fantasies of self and others. Especially because trauma paralyzes and overwhelms, we must not lose sight of the way individuals *play an active though not always conscious role* in perceiving, organizing and responding to their experience.

Understanding that traumatizing childhood experiences are events that happens *to* the patient *but are also* a process of active engagement, changes the way we think about trauma. It helps us focus on determinants of how the trauma is organized in the patient's mind: the heart of what the trauma *means* to the person. Accessing the patient's core fantasies is critical to this understanding. It also points us to processes that are actively under patients' control, processes they *can* do something about. This is essential because trauma involves so much that the survivor is unable to do anything about.

We cannot go back and change the reality of loss, abuse and neglect. But we can stay aware of what we are communicating to our patients through our own words, tone, actions and modes of relating to them. If we focus only on trauma as an event, or on the *content* of the patient's experience, we may be unwittingly distracting patients from the *process* of how they are organizing the trauma—how they are making meaning of what happened to them. What fantasies are stimulated by the early experience? Do they use the abuse to reinforce or reconnect with a sense of helplessness? Do they deaden themselves to avoid psychic pain? Do they seek out similar situations in attempts at mastery or because of difficulties separating from early modes of relating? Do they engage the trauma they experienced with determination to re-order priorities? Do they find some sort of desire fulfilled by getting caught up in experiencing themselves as a victim? A focus on complex developmental trauma as *process* enables patients to re-engage seeing themselves as active agents in their own lives. The importance of this cannot be overestimated. Listening for how patients are organizing their experience, how they are fantasizing about it, how they are relating to it, how they are hiding from it, in essence, *how they are using it*, is an essential aspect of helping them to reconnect with the active aspect of themselves.

CHAPTER 6

Transference/Countertransference

We have spoken of transference as a special subset of the fantasizing activity that characterizes all experience. *Transference is relatedness revived, expressed and symbolized in the therapeutic interaction.* Transference activity is ubiquitous, always present, operative in all experience. It is part of the mental activity we become more aware of through the therapeutic process. Transference activity brings the process of how relatedness is organized into the immediacy of the therapeutic moment. It is uniquely present, infused with the wishes and fears, expectations and actions that organize our world and make us who we are. Transference is central in therapeutic work because it arises from and captures the core emotional relatedness that motivates experience. Within the unique asymmetrical structure of the therapeutic situation, where we are primarily involved with a focus on explicating the patient's inner world, exploring the patient's transference activity enables us to better understand the complex interpersonal dynamics that are emerging in the interpersonal domain. These dynamics are fueled by fantasized wishes and fears connected to powerful

emotional currents. Within the unique structure of the therapeutic situation, transference activity can be examined with an
emotional connectedness that talking about interaction rarely
achieves. The identification and analysis of transference activity is prized because it allows the participants to gain direct
knowledge of emotionally based patterns of thought, feeling,
defense and action. This direct experience moves the treatment
from talking about content to uncovering the emotionally felt,
underlying organization that guides all experience.

Each participant brings his or her unique configuration
of fantasy and transference activity to the therapeutic process.
When the focus is on what the patient's inner world brings to the
interaction, we speak about the patient's transference. When the
therapist reflects on the inner wishes, feelings and fantasies
that are stimulated by the patient and the interaction, we speak
about the therapist's countertransference. Both participants
bring their idiosyncratic mental organization to the treatment
process, but the interaction, the intersubjective space between
the collaborators, is mutually constructed (Adler and Bachant,
1998). Therapy focuses on the transference of the patient, the
way that the countertransference of the therapist provides clues
to patterns of emergent relatedness, and the way in which both
collaborators contribute to constructing the interaction.

Transference/countertransference activity is accorded a
special place in psychotherapy because it gives form and sub-
stance to the relatedness between patient and therapist, *where it
can be analyzed, examined, explored and understood.* We use a powerful interpersonal tool to uncover an understanding of how the
patient organizes experience. What makes transference analysis so useful is that it brings mental organization *along with
its affective component* into the heart of the therapeutic process.
Speaking of the erotic in the broadest sense, Freud described

the situation eloquently—only transference renders "the ines-
timable service of making the patient's buried and forgotten
erotic impulses immediate and manifest" (Freud, 1912, p. 108).
In the direct immediacy of their encounter, transference/coun-
tertransference activity engages both participants in a process
that moves toward action. In Freud's (1914) noteworthy paper,
Remembering, Repeating and Working Through, he comments that

> the patient does not *remember* anything of what he has
> forgotten and repressed, but *acts* it out. He reproduces it
> not as a memory but as an action: he *repeats* it, without, of
> course, knowing that he is repeating it (Freud, 1914, p. 150,
> italics in the original).

These actions take many forms that range from the scarcely
noticeable to those that threaten to derail the treatment. Understanding the range of transference-based enactments enables us
to find opportunities to meaningfully explore the most intimate
kinds of relating: within oneself and with others.

Transference activity involves an *inner dimension*, (preformed expectations, modes of relating, wishes, fears, conflicts
and moral imperatives that are brought to the relationship by
each participant) as well as an *intersubjective dimension* (interpersonal engagement with a separate person). Most of the time,
transference activity operates rather silently, always present
but in the background of the patient's immediate concerns.
Transference infuses attachments and identifications that are
valued aspects of the patient's self-image, as well as modes of
relating to self and others that patients may want to change.
Transference carries mental organization in relatedness. As
therapists, we may be only semi-aware of its presence, noticing it only when unmetabolized, unintegrated transference

impulses intrude on the process. We may sense its emergence, for example, when we experience an aggressive impulse with a masochistic patient, when we sense that an erotic element is starting to infuse the interaction, or when we anticipate with dread a patient's demand that we provide them with better service. In this way, examining transference/countertransference activity offers us the possibility of using the relationship to find core organizing activity.

Learning to work in the transference does not happen automatically and sometimes is confounding. How do we identify transference activity? How quickly should we move to transference engagement and interpretations? How do we resolve transference projections that threaten the relationship? How do we "develop" the transference without getting hijacked by it? When do we ask the patient if what they have been talking about has some reference to our relationship? What can we do to "deepen" transference engagement? How and when do we use our own countertransference activity to identify and engage the patient's transference activity?

Much has been written about working with transference and countertransference that is important reading. *In essence, transference is relatedness embodied.* This relatedness has its roots in important, meaningful interactions in the patient's past—in the bio/psycho/social determinants of experience. It is relatedness that is revived, expressed and symbolized in the therapeutic interaction. I want to emphasize here that the essence of transference work involves having the courage to explore, examine and analyze transference activity as it is represented in the therapeutic interaction. Transference activity can be represented in fantasies, actions, enactments, wishes and fears, bodily experiences as well as relatedness to self and others. We can see transference with a client who anticipates with fear that the therapist (or other people) will be angry when he is doing what he wants rather than what the other expects. In a similar vein with a patient who asks for reassurance in words or actions, we can turn our attention to that process with non-judgmental curiosity, rather than countertransferentially complying with the patient's wish. It can be fundamentally much more reassuring to help patients understand why they want to turn to another or why they cannot reassure themselves than to gratify the patient's unconscious wish. This examination of the process tells patients that we are truly interested in their inner life. We desire to fully know them.

Transference engagements are routinely enacted before we become aware of them. The key is to identify the enacted aspect of the interaction and then to use that awareness along with our nonjudgmental curiosity to open up the process. The value of working with the smallest manifestations of transference activity is that it moves the exploration into an area that is most meaningful to the patient and does so at a time when patients have the psychic room to reflect on their experience. The ability to maintain an observing ego while examining unintegrated psychic material is especially important for patients who have experienced complex developmental trauma. These patients can become so immersed in early, emotionally loaded feelings and beliefs that they lose a vital connection to the more centered aspects of self. Uncovering the details of the patient's fantasies about our relatedness to them while their observing ego functions are intact, tends to mitigate transference storms through reflective engagement with the patient's inner world. This reflection stimulates archaic longings, irrational fears and deep-seated conflicts. Exploring the details of the patient's transference activity involves giving patients the room and respect to reflect on their experience.

Edith came into the session talking about how overloaded she is for the next month, at work, helping her husband, having her daughter back from college, needing to go on work related trips, see friends, etc. Although it did sound daunting, and I could empathize with her sense of being up against it, there was a quality in *how* she was telling me about what she was facing that reverberated inside me.

Is she really this overwhelmed? If so, despite the reality of the events she described, where does this feeling come from? I had the distinct impression that Edith was asking for something from me. There was a quality of imploring me, of wanting me to take pity on her or to show sympathy for her predicament. I felt that she was trying to show me something that she wanted me to see. I told her that I could see that she had a lot on her plate and that the next month was going to be very taxing, but that I was also wondering about the feeling that was in the room. I told her that I wasn't sure what was going on, but that I had the sense that she was talking about more than the events that were crowding into her life. I wondered out loud if there was some way in which feeling overwhelmed was important to her, maybe important for her to show me. Maybe this way of relating to herself and to me had something to tell us.

Immediately, Edith told me that she HATED feeling this way. It made her feel horrible and tense all the time, and not able to look forward to anything. But then she paused and told me that as a child she was always busy, busy, busy. Always engaged with projects and school work, and cheerleading, and music, and didn't remember feeling overwhelmed in the way that she did now. I asked her how long she had been having feelings like this and she told me that she thought they had started after her youngest child went off to school. She thought about this for a moment and put up her hand facing me, and then turned it so it faced herself. "I think there was a turn at that point, where I had to look at myself . . . and that makes me anxious." *"Anxious?" I asked.* "Yes, when I was so busy with school, and work and projects, and later with the kids, I didn't have to look inside. It was easier. Safer." She paused and teared up. "Now, I wonder if I make myself feel overwhelmed so that I can comfort myself. I think I only allow myself to comfort myself if I'm overwhelmed."

Edith's reflections on this experience were brought to the fore by the traces of emotional activation I could feel being enacted in our transference relationship, in her imploring way of presenting herself to me. Noticing this enactment collaboratively and encouraging examination of it enabled us to more fully explore her anxiety about looking inside, her difficulty comforting herself without first feeling overwhelmed, and her preference to relate (to herself and to me) through situations of being overburdened.

CHAPTER 7

Resistance

Freud defined resistance as "whatever interrupts the progress of analytic work" (Freud, 1900, p. 517). But we must bear in mind that in addition to impeding therapeutic process, resistances, like all psychological processes, serve multiple functions. Resistance, for example, can protect us from painful feelings, express or enact unconscious fantasies, preserve our relationship to significant others, enact self punitive and self-sabotaging impulses, conserve central relational patterns, express the motivational power of guilt and shame, maintain psychological homeostasis, and, perhaps most importantly, protect our autonomy, identity and self-cohesion from impingements that could be destabilizing (Adler and Bachant, 1998).

Therapists of most persuasions understand that resistance is expressed in every session. This is inevitable because entering therapy is an acknowledgement that patients want to change, and we are inescapably conflicted about wanting to change. Early in life we develop an internal psychic framework, a set of fundamental ideas, wishes, fears and modes of relating that becomes an enduring mental framework that structures inner and outer experiencing. This framework is useful, essential in many ways because it is adaptive: it allows us to make predictions and adjustments to our world without having to reinvent ourselves anew with every changing circumstance. We need to understand, however, that this mental framework is the product of a mind that was organized with early right hemisphere emotional dominance and immature cognitive functions. The ideas, fantasies, beliefs and patterns of relating that are structured into our mental framework are often branded with the emotional conviction of right brain functioning and unconscious infantile misconceptions (Ginot, 2015). Shadowing the desire for change lurks a powerful fear of even small modifications to this early psychic organization. This mental framework represents the best possible equilibrium we were able to develop in the face of multiple, conflicting psychological forces. Even the wish to alter the structure of our early psychic organization can feel like jumping into the abyss. It is no wonder that Freud (1915) described resistance as inevitably accompanying the treatment step by step.

Resistance, then, is the guardian of psychic equilibrium. As such, the patient has an enormous investment in keeping it going (Adler and Bachant, 1998; Rangell, 1983; Freud, 1937; Fenichel, 1941; Greenson, 1967). This might sound discouraging, but the opposite is true. Resistance is one of the most significant achievements of childhood, generating early childhood "strategies" that provide us with protective functions that last into adulthood.

Resistance guards psychic equilibrium in times perceived as dangerous. The strategies developed to protect our emotional balance are many and varied, ranging from defenses that are automatic and unconscious to temporary adjustments that are instituted until an improved solution can be substituted or those to which we are intensely committed. It is only from an external vantage point that resistance or the development of defense will seem unnecessary, contrary, or constrictive. We must also remember that anything can be used in the service of defense. Whereas clinicians used to think that there were a limited number of specific defense mechanisms, we now understand that people operate in a much more global fashion, enlisting any mental function at hand (thinking, feeling, fantasy, actions) in the service of defense and resistance (Brenner, 1982). This way of thinking becomes important as we help patients understand their attachment to childhood strategies that have outlived their usefulness. We will examine defense in more detail in the section *Listening for the Footprints of the Past*. Resistance is a creative inner process that has helped people navigate turbulent times. It can be respected and valued as an important developmental tool, one that enabled us to function when emotionally challenged.

Working with resistance, therefore is immensely valuable to the therapist as it points us directly to the patient's core issues. Resistance provides us with a map of the uncharted territory of the patient's fears, fantasies and conflicts. It is to be welcomed rather than dreaded, "befriended" rather than pushed away (Van der Kolk, 2015). Very often, resistance is tied to trauma and the strategies developed to deal with early emotional problems, revealing a creative and courageous desire to protect the self. Central to working with resistance is an appreciation of this history. When patients tell us they want to change but have trouble making it happen, we work to uncover the emotional investment they have in maintaining behaviors they tell us they want to modify. This can be tricky, as some patients find it hard to believe that they are committed to maintaining a behavior that causes them suffering. We help them to understand this paradoxical reality by uncovering the details and the meaning of their subjective experience within the therapeutic situation. Activating our curiosity is an essential element in being able to ask the relevant questions: What emotions are being warded off? What threat to psychic equilibrium is anticipated? What protections are invoked? What does the belief in a guilty self purchase for the patient? What relationship in fantasy is being conserved? How is the therapist's behavior viewed by the patient?

Resistance shadows the therapeutic process at every step, but we can learn to use it as an ally in the treatment. It is one of our most powerful tools because once it is understood, it helps patients make sense of their experience. The pieces of the puzzle begin to fit together.

CHAPTER 8

Multiple Functioning

To understand how trauma affects development we have to have a framework to organize in our own minds the complexity of mental functioning itself. The human brain is the most complex of all biological organs. Like the stars, what is visible to us, (what we can be conscious of) is only a tiny fraction of what is there. Edelman (2004) tells us that if you start counting synapses at a rate of one per second, it would take 32 million years to finish! Our brains not only give rise to consciousness but also mediate our emotional and behavioral responses. The structure of the brain, its higher cognitive functions, and its core emotional systems are the products of evolutionary history (Panksepp, 1998; Stefansson, 2007), wired in for efficiency and flexibility. Most of our mental processing, therefore, is unconscious. How, then, can we organize our thinking about mental functioning and psychological development so that we have a better grasp of what is going on in the minds of other people?

In this section, we will explore the nature of the forces that influence development and mental functioning and organize them into three domains: biological, psychological and social determinants. Second, we will examine the principle of multiple function. Finally, we will underscore the importance of keeping in mind the individual uniqueness of each person's inner life.

The Bio/Psycho/Social Determinants of Mental Functioning

Whenever we ask ourselves the question, "Why on earth did he do that?" we are asking about what determines a person's choices. There are always many reasons we unconsciously consider in order to arrive at the experience of feeling, thinking or acting in a specific manner. We are always synthesizing an enormous amount of data from our inner and outer experience.

Barbara is a woman whose choice of husband was determined by her experience of being rescued from illness by her mother when she was an infant and being hated by her older sister for stealing their mother's attention. These two factors loom very large in Barbara's psychology, but they are not the only determinants of her behavior. There are always many. In therapy, it is our job to help patients understand themselves better, but how do we make sense and order out of the countless things patients say and do? One of the strategies that many therapists use is to organize the determinants of experience into three broad, manageable categories: biological factors, psychological factors and social factors—the biopsychosocial model. This model sees behavior and experience as affected by multiple levels of organization, from the molecular to the cultural (Borrell-Carrio, Suchman & Epstein, 2004). Keeping in mind that each of these factors has some influence on the patient's experience helps us not to get stuck in a one-dimensional picture of the patient's world.

Biological Factors

Biological determinants of a person's experience exist on a continuum from readily observable to hidden from others. The color of a person's eyes or skin, an individual's height, whether they were born with a physical abnormality, such as a club foot, a concave chest, or an extra finger are characteristics that are readily observable. Other biological factors are veiled, so that they are not easily seen. An example of this kind of biological factor is the threshold for anxiety that a person is born with. We know now that the tendency to be anxious is determined by a mixture of genetic factors. Children who get many of these factors will have a low threshold for anxiety, meaning that they will tend to become anxious rather easily. Children who inherit only a few of these anxiety producing genes will take more to make them anxious — we can say that these children have a high tolerance for anxiety, or a higher threshold for anxiety. Ability to tolerate frustration, introversion/extraversion, mood, sensitiveness, and adaptability are qualities of temperament that are considered to have a biological substrate. Another biological factor that is not initially observable is the genetic heritability of mental illness. Schizophrenia and bipolar disorder are genetic disorders that are difficult to diagnose until the person is manifesting overt symptoms, usually in late adolescence or early adulthood. Their influence may be hidden for many years. Biological factors, such as a tendency toward depression, can directly influence how a person thinks, feels and relates to others. Additionally, there are always interactions with the environment that can modulate or accentuate biological factors. Physical pain, for example, especially when experienced as a child, from surgery, accidents or medical procedures can have powerful influences on the development of defenses, fantasy and coping strategies. Biological determinants can influence experience directly or indirectly.

Social Factors

Social causes of mental organization include the larger influence of cultural norms as well as the more intimate determinants of how one is related to in the family of origin. There are countless socially mediated experiences that influence the child's development. A parent's ability or inability to emotionally engage the child will have profound impact on the child's emotional and social development. The presence of a loving grandma in a family that is otherwise emotionally distant can be a lifeline for a struggling child. Other examples of social factors that influence the child's development are the parent's capacity for loving attachment, actions of their siblings and family members, the ability of the parents or caregivers to verbalize emotional experience, neglect or abuse of the child, as well as the communication of social norms and cultural values, such as valuing achievement or family connections. We are engineered by evolution to be social animals, creatures for whom connection to others is necessary for survival. Social factors are often the first factors one thinks about when considering motivation. Explanations such as, "she wasn't loved as a child, so she neglects her own child's needs," or "his family didn't value education, so he never wanted to go to college," may contain part of the truth, but they oversimplify a complex situation that has many variables. With my patient Barbara, both the devotion of her mother during Barbara's early illness and the hatred of her sister were social determinants of her psychological organization. Her experience would look very different had she been a first-born child, or if her sister had more ability to tolerate the loss of their mother. Our current lives and our histories are replete with social factors that contribute to the way we think and feel.

Psychological Factors

I have saved for last the influence on mental development of psychological factors because these features markedly affect the significance of both biological and social factors. The domain of psychological factors encompasses the way the individual perceives biological and social realities, the meaning given to experience. Psychological factors are crucial in understanding motivation. How the person *interprets* biological and social forces makes the difference between seeing a traumatic accident as confirming a sense of victimhood—"bad things always happen to me," "I just have bad luck," "you can't escape your fate"—versus seeing the accident as a challenge to endure, an opportunity to rise above the crisis or even to help others. Even identical twins, raised in the same family, will interpret their experience differently. Likewise, we cannot assume that what was good (or bad) for us as children will have the same effect on our own children. The enormous complexity and uniqueness of each person's bio/psycho/social determinants must always be kept in mind. Generalizations are not helpful.

In the case of Barbara, for example, although we talked about the social factors involved (the powerful influence of the early devotion of her mother nursing her out of illness, and the role of her sister, who was very resentful of how their mother abandoned her in order to care for Barbara), we did not talk about the psychological factors that emerged *inside* Barbara –the way she organized these social influences. A major psychological determinant for Barbara was how she brought punishment into her mode of relating to self and others. Punishment was a primary factor in Barbara's psychology. Punishment and sadomasochistic enactments played a large role in her sexual life, in her interactions with others in and out of the transference and of course in how she related to herself. Unconsciously, Barbara punished herself for being an Oedipal victor (winning the mother), for being alive when she was supposed to die, as well as through an identification with the aggression of her older sister. Punishment simultaneously gratified her sister's aggressive wishes and returned her to being the victimized child that called out for her mother's care.

Self-punishment is a very common psychological factor that must be unraveled for the best treatment outcome. It is generally unconscious and needs to be excavated from transference enactments and from examining how patients relate to themselves and others. Self-punishment is a psychological factor that has its roots in the way the patient perceives, organizes and integrates social and biological influences. Without understanding the importance of psychological factors on development, we cannot obtain a comprehensive understanding of a person's mental functioning.

> It is not unusual for couples who have tried unsuccessfully for years to have a child, first to adopt one and only then be able to conceive. Maggie was 14 months old when her mother gave birth to a baby girl. Unable to talk, she could only communicate her distress with tearful, incoherent rages. Her parents clearly loved both children, but Maggie developed the idea that her parents brought another child into the family *because she was bad*. Her sister was the golden child, all sunny disposition and blond curls. Maggie was dark haired and dark tempered—so different from the other family members. Maggie organized her

sister's arrival as having the meaning that she was not good enough, that being different was dangerous, that she was inherently bad, and that it was for these reasons that her parents brought another child into the family. Maggie's parents loved her. But the way Maggie organized the facts of her childhood led her to a very different conclusion. These childhood fantasies, which coalesced into firmly held beliefs over time, had a far-reaching impact on Maggie's ability to function intrapsychically and interpersonally. When she began treatment, she was so profoundly disconnected from herself that she had no idea who she was. She married a man she didn't love and couldn't connect with simply because he wanted her. She knew very little about what she truly wanted or enjoyed. Maggie, a very intelligent, creative, imaginative woman, had spent the first fifty years of her life living as a shadow of herself.

When we talk about psychological factors, we need to be aware that it is not only the facts that are important. What is especially crucial is how the person *interprets* those facts, the *meaning* they are making from their experiences. Essential in understanding the forces at work in our patient's minds is the realization that the person who interprets these early facts of life is a child. Childhood interpretations and childhood strategies with the problems of living are formed during a time when the child's cognitive functioning has not yet matured. The wishes, fears, fantasies, ideas and thoughts that come to shape psychological experience are imprinted with a child's logic and understanding. Nevertheless, these early modes of thinking and relating become structured into the individual's mental maps. They become activated automatically and are usually unconscious.

The meaning children make of their life circumstances and emotional dilemmas is often hidden from others, even from parents. It is often hidden from the children themselves. Psychological determinants are the most important and difficult to uncover because they are stealthy, like a virus that invades the body's cells. Very often, the child is totally unaware of these ideas and fantasies and communicates them to no one. They exist more in unconscious actions and inner dialogue than anywhere else. Uncovering and developing the *meaning* that patients are making from the therapist's actions, their actions, or the actions or words of others will help us help them more fully understand their motivation.

It is largely because the psychological determinants of experience can never be completely known that understanding a person's motivation is so difficult. Each domain, the biological, the social and the psychological, brings countless forces to bear on development as the individual seeks to work out an integration of what are often conflicting aims. Mind and brain are continually engaged in synthesizing information from outer and inner domains. This synthesizing process happens automatically and largely unconsciously. It is the reason why if you have to make a big and difficult decision, it is often better to sleep on it than to make a list of the pros and cons.

Human life is too multifaceted and too complex to be reduced to simple one to one correspondences. We cannot say that because a parent encourages diligence and academic performance their children will grow up to perform well academically, just as we cannot say that parents who discourage academic pursuits will not have a child that loves the intellectual life. There are simply too many factors involved in mental functioning for simplistic explanations to hold true.

But we can go even further in thinking about the many layers of mental processing that interact to determine experience. In addition to the biopsychosocial determinants of experience, every act, thought, symptom or fear can also serve multiple *functions*. It can gratify multiple internal needs. In the case of Barbara, for example, her masochism served the function of both punishing herself for her aggressive wishes toward her sister and simultaneously crying out to her mother for help. Robert Waelder (1936) developed the principle of multiple function, the idea that psychological symptoms simultaneously relieve conflict and are caused by conflict. Phobias, compulsions, defenses, even preferred modes of relating in the world have multiple internal aspects that influence whether and how they will be expressed. Brenner (1982) described the mind as continually involved in developing compromise formations, the observable aspects of psychic functioning that are a compromise between anxiety and misery, defense and moral considerations. As we do psychotherapy, we need to keep in mind that every action, every thought, every feeling, every experience a person has is determined by multiple forces. Without having to think about it, we generate a formula that best balances the multiple forces at work in our minds. When we realize that these multiple determinants are organized primarily unconsciously, we stand humbled by the sheer complexity of the processing that goes into the simplest action.

Because of this complexity, we must always keep in mind that we cannot generalize about behavior, symptoms, motivation or personality. People combine bio/psycho/social forces into patterns of thinking, feeling, behaving and relating that are uniquely their own *and* that serve multiple functions for them. People not familiar with how the mind works routinely ask therapists to make judgements about what a certain behavior means or from what it is derived. But we cannot assume that a person who is critical and judgmental had critical parents. Or that people who are sadistic had abusive parents. Or that people who are always helping others are kind—kindness may be one dimension of their experience, but they might also be kind in order to compensate for inner rage and aggression that they find intolerable to acknowledge. Instead, we must always hold dear the understanding that without a lot of information about an individual's bio/psycho/social history, as well as their current functioning, we can't generalize about them at all. Mental functioning is too complex to reduce to a scant number of variables. We help ourselves, our patients and our profession when we put into practice the notion that, when it comes to explaining human experience, every understanding is by definition only a partial understanding.

PART III

Therapeutic Skills: Listening for the Footprints of the Past

"It is only with the heart that one can see rightly; what is essential is invisible to the eye."
— Antoine de Saint-Exupery, *The Little Prince*

All therapists know that listening is crucial to therapeutic effectiveness. Listening encourages the patient to communicate their mental organization to us and also creates a space for reflection. Our listening enables the patient to be heard. We are professionally trained to listen carefully not only to the content and the feelings that emerge in sessions, but also to the many layers of meaning in *how* patients communicate with us. Therapeutic listening is fundamentally about listening with the heart—understanding meanings, feelings, and how patients' minds are organized. Only by understanding what certain actions, ideas, feelings and fantasies *mean* can we understand and ultimately help this unique individual. To develop this understanding, we must learn to listen for the details that provide context and for the patient's subjective perspective in the therapeutic situation.

Perhaps the most overarching challenge in listening to patients with histories of complex developmental trauma is the need to alter our thinking about authority. Even though the patient is coming to us for help, even though we are perceived as the expert, therapeutic listening involves listening with the understanding that our experience of the patient is necessarily limited. Listening with the appreciation that *ultimate authority lies with the patient* is respectful, analytic listening. We need to listen to the patient with humility, respect and nonjudgmental curiosity. The deepest and most intense treatment can only begin to understand the complexity of forces operating on the patient. It is listening that enables one to hear the heart of fantasy, transference and enactments. This kind of listening is critically important when working with those who have experienced childhood losses, abuse or neglect, because childhood trauma alters patients' psychological equilibrium and makes them vulnerable to relinquishing autonomy and control. When traumatized, we want to be safe and, often, to be taken care of. Although patients may need to be taken care of in the immediate aftermath of a trauma, our goal is to help patients restore autonomy and control in their own lives. To further integration, we focus on helping patients synthesize the forces at work in *their psyches*, rather than in *our ideas* which can only approximate the complexity of forces operative in their minds. Only the patient is privy to the unique and complex balance of the bio/psycho/social forces that guides psychological functioning. Only the patient can determine what is possible at any given time. Considerations of tact, timing and plausibility are especially critical in working with traumatized patients; a more directive approach can undermine the patient's growing ability to reclaim personal agency.

With this overarching framework of respect that ultimate authority lies with the patient, therapeutic listening can proceed with listening for the latent wishes, fears, ideas and fantasies that organize experience. Fundamentally, we are listening for unconscious activity, the dissociated inner voices that have been pushed aside. The following chapters outline the many ways that latent content is revealed: in the content, feelings, defense, transference/countertransference, meaning, enactments and organization the patient brings to each session. Every session has micro-manifestations of these processes ready to be mined. We can access unconscious processes in many ways: by attending to sequencing, symbolic representation, slips of the tongue, tracking the patient's associations, checking in with our own feelings, fantasies and associations, examining enactments, attending to posture, tone of voice, dreams, overall organizing themes, and, most importantly, to how the patient relates to us. When working with trauma patients, we are very interested in *how* patients say things, which gives us clues to warded off mental contents.

We need to remember that unintegrated aspects are not conscious for important reasons. These reasons may be preverbal—relational trauma that occurred so early in life that the child was unable to organize the experience in words.

They may be intolerably painful. They may conceal wishes that are frightening. They may involve attachment needs, defenses or impulses to disconnect from their own experience in order to satisfy inner or outer demands. With patients who have suffered chronic traumatizing emotional adversity in childhood, unintegrated aspects of self are often carried in the body. These split off aspects of self carry fears or fantasies that are raw. Asking the patient to give voice to these embodied feelings and fears is a technique that can reach otherwise inaccessible mental contents. "See if you can hear what that choked up knot in your stomach is saying." "What is that stabbing pain in your heart telling us?" Asking the patient to draw a family portrait is a technique that Van der Kolk (2014) uses to allow patients to express early relatedness. This technique allows the patient to express through their bodies by their drawings, what they may not be able to allow themselves to see or know consciously.

The defenses connected with split off aspects of self typically involve representations of caretaking or protections that patients feel they cannot live without.

Working through these defenses begins by acknowledging their importance, understanding how they protected the child's earliest experience of self.

Fundamentally we need to understand the child's investment in creating a safe environment, even at the cost of disconnecting from the self.

Later in the work, patients can be helped to see the connections between their current problems in living and what were originally developed as "solutions" to the problems of their childhoods. Throughout treatment we also need to be uncovering the hidden gratifications that make these defensive solutions continue to seem worthwhile.

As we listen for content, sequence, affect, symbolic allusions, metaphor, tonal inflections and bodily expression, we are always staying connected to, thinking about, and feeling through what the patient is wanting from us. Listening for transferential activity can be elusive. It can feel easier, safer, and less challenging to stay with the content level of understanding. But over a hundred years of reflecting on therapeutic work has taught us that focusing on how patients see and interact with us, and especially what they want from us, helps us to connect directly to their latent content. It can be a shortcut to deeper understanding. Does the patient want us (or the treatment) to produce high quality results in the way their father demanded results of them? Do they want the comfort and understanding of a caring mother or grandparent? Do they want to be punished for daring to have their own needs and ideas? Do they want the recognition that eluded them in childhood? To prove that they are indeed attractive? How patients organize what they want from us and from the treatment helps us to elicit their deepest dynamic issues. Listening for what the patient is wanting from us is augmented by listening to the voices inside ourselves that convey our countertransferential impulses—feelings, thoughts and fantasies that can clue us in to the process of our interaction.

The ability to hear the footsteps from the past, especially the unconscious processes that represent traumatic experience, is the heart of dynamic psychotherapy. Grasping the organization that motivates experience is an essential part of deepening the work. Hearing in this special way requires a type of listening that is a complex, highly disciplined skill, very different from ordinary communication. Essentially, this type of listening involves uncovering the many layers of meaning and structure that infuse the patient's verbal and nonverbal communications.

These listening skills require intricate interaction between perceiving the patient and perceiving the therapist's own inner processes. Personal experience in psychotherapy is indispensable in developing the best handle on these skills.

For teaching purposes, I have organized these layers of listening into separate categories. When dealing with an actual person's experience, such divisions often blend into each other. For simplicity's sake, however, we will structure the basic layers as listening for: content, feeling, defense, transference/countertransference, meaning, enactment, and organization. Our focus in this section is on listening skills, hearing the multiple ways that traces of enduring forms of emotional adversity are represented in the dialogue between patient and therapist. Learning what to listen for and how developmental trauma can be represented helps therapists better formulate both their understanding of the patient and how they should proceed.

CHAPTER 9

Listening for Content

Attend to *What* the Patient is Saying

Listening for content is generally the first skill that beginning therapists learn. When we listen for content, we are listening for the thoughts and facts of people's experience; we are listening to the story that they are telling us. What are they trying to communicate? Does their narrative make sense? Is it told abstractly or with detail? Is it consistent or do we feel that there are missing parts? Are we on the same page as the patient in understanding what he or she is explaining?

The act of being truly and deeply listened to is a profound gift that some patients have never experienced before. It is very different from being told what they should be doing, how they should be doing it or what the therapist thinks the problem is. They have heard all that—many times. As we develop our ability to listen to and reflect on the content of the patient's communication, our respect, curiosity and nonjudgmental interest can stimulate a deepening of the patient's experience of being listened to, and further associations, memories, wishes, fears and fantasies can begin to emerge for exploration. This important shift can occur when patients begin to feel that they are being heard and seen for who they truly are.

Practice Paraphrasing the Content

Paraphrasing the content gives us preparation in following and empathizing with the patient's experience. It opens a door that allows other types of mental contents to come to the fore. Good paraphrasing is not parroting back what the patient has said. Ideally, paraphrasing captures the *essence* of what the patient says in different words, letting the patient know that you really understand the thoughts and facts being communicated. Paraphrases should be *short* and *focused* on the essential message the patient is communicating. Young (2009, p. 129) describes a two step process in paraphrasing:

1. Listen carefully to the patient's story and then
2. Feed back to the patient a condensed, nonjudgmental version of the facts and thoughts.

Practice paraphrasing the content until it feels easy for you to do.

PT: *My father and mother have been living with us since my son was born, almost a year now. I am having a lot of trouble with the way my father wants everything done his way. I respect my father and want to be a good son, but I am not a child anymore.*

T: *You're having some difficulties living with your parents and you are not sure that your father sees you as an adult.*

Develop the Ability to Reflect the Content

We learn to hone our listening skills by *reflecting what the patient is saying,* implicitly asking the patient to correct us if we are off track. Listening for content enables us to establish rapport with our patients and refine the accuracy of our understanding. We need not worry about being perfectly in tune with the patient. A "good enough" listener will be just fine because we will always be checking in with the patient to make sure that our hypotheses are on the right track. If we sense that important pieces of information are missing, it is vital to bring that to the patient's attention. Remarks can be made such as "I'm confused. Would you go over that again?" or "I think I missed something here. How did you get from talking about your girlfriend to talking about your father?" Even if our perception of what the patient has told us is very off base, the important thing is to be open to being corrected, to establish an atmosphere of collaboration where the patient knows that we are invested in knowing him or her as accurately as possible. *This collaborative atmosphere also serves the function of helping the patient to invest more fully in the process* rather than simply turning himself over to the therapist's authority.

Learning to reflect content involves asking and being able to answer the question: "Who is doing what to whom?"

CHAPTER 10

Listening for Feeling

Communication is always multifaceted and uses a range of modalities. One of the most important aspects for the therapist to listen for is the thread of feeling that the patient conveys in the tapestry of what she says and how she says it. Panksepp (1998); Damasio (1994, 1999, 2003), and LeDoux (1996) suggest that affect is the basis of mind and the foundation of cognition. Solms (2013) adds that consciousness is inherently affective, that affect is an intrinsic property of the brain. The threads of feeling that weave in and out of verbal and nonverbal communications are central to knowing oneself and other selves. Subjectivity and intersubjectivity are rooted in our feeling-based relatedness, and especially in the feeling-based mental patterns that are organized from the beginning of life. Psychotherapy is fundamentally emotionally based. If the feeling component is not developed, the treatment remains on the surface. Emotional connection is vital to a successful outcome.

Browning (2019) maintains that our capacity to feel is at the heart of consciousness and relatedness, driving action and symbolic functioning. Following the seminal work of Deacon (1997) and Langer (1953, 1967, 1988), and alongside the contemporary work of Damasio (1994, 1999, 2003); LeDoux (1996); Solms (2013), and Panksepp (1998), Browning contends that the development of the human mind is based on a core affective subjectivity. Feeling is at the heart of consciousness. Feeling is what we mean by consciousness and is the driving force in the development of our mental lives. Browning suggests that the *projection of affect* allows us to formulate ideas with others about our common objective world and to organize and reorganize our personal subjective worlds. "Not only do we share an explicitly common external world, but we . . . develop our internal worlds in this intersubjective theatre with others" (Browning, 2019, p. 28).

Feeling is manifest in words, actions, movements, quality of eye contact, tone of voice, facial expressions, posture, verbal rhythms, and especially in symbolic representations. Early organization, memories and fantasies are often manifest in symbolic enactments with the therapist. Freud's (1900) early advice to follow the affect as a way to access core motivational dynamics remains as relevant now as it was more than a hundred years ago. As we listen to patients, we need to work to identify, examine and explore these representations of feeling.

Feelings can be consonant with the content of the patient's narrative or they can be very different. A patient speaking about the death of his father may talk about loss, but underneath the content may be a simmering rage or resentment that he doesn't allow himself to think about. We might access these deeper feelings by noting the disconnectedness of his expression, or our own feelings of boredom or disconnectedness, or a tone that is more appropriate to resentment than loss. *If we stay only with the content, we miss helping the patient to own and acknowledge a primary connection to himself and the complexity of his experience.* Being unaware of underlying feelings often leads to them being expressed or acted out in ways that can be problematic. Focusing on the feeling level of the patient's narrative gives the patient an opportunity to connect with warded off experience. Feelings play a significant role in the structuring of experience. Logic and reason have important roles to play as well, but feeling states are at the heart of what motivates us, what moves us. Emotion is built into our subcortical neural systems, providing us with a foundation through which we can explore other minds and our own subjectivity (LeDoux, 1998; Panksepp, 1998). Even people who are profoundly debilitated by major mental illnesses often retain the ability to connect accurately through feeling (Damasio, 1994; Sacks, 1985).

Feeling can also be noticed in its absence. When a patient talks about the trauma of discovering his wife has been having an affair, he may be numb with shock, unable to connect with his grief in a direct way. We may have to stay with the patient in his shock or rage before he is able to access his sadness. In a similar way, patients who have been abused often disconnect from feelings of rage and betrayal. Noticing a lack of feeling is just as instructive as noticing a particular feeling. It is a signpost on the road to unexplored territory.

Attend to the Feeling Component of the Patient's Expression

Feelings are manifest in many ways: The simple statement, "She asked me to take out the garbage again," can carry a tone that communicates guilt, rage, irritation, sheepishness, a whole gamut of different feelings. Our first task is to *identify the feeling* using tone, intensity and other nonverbal cues to hone our understanding most accurately. Is the feeling a subtle breeze or a threatening storm of emotion? As we listen to the content of the patient's narrative, we try to identify the primary emotion that infuses the story. Is it one of frustration? Shame? Guilt? Rage? Fear? Joy? Sadness? We have talked about the way that feelings can be used defensively against other feelings, and this can complicate matters as more than one feeling may be present. But as we listen for the feeling tone of the patient's narrative, we want to listen for the patient's deepest, most authentic feeling. Very often, for example, rage is used to defend against the awareness of sadness and hurt, as in the case of the patient who reported saying in a conversation with his wife, "All you care about is yourself!" to hide an intense sadness about not feeling loved.

Ideally, the therapist's reflections of feeling are integrated with reflections of content. Reflections of feeling tell the patient that you have understood how they are emotionally affected by what they are telling you. The first step is to *identify* the patient's feelings. The second step is to *communicate* to the patient the underlying emotions that we have discerned. For example, "When your daughter doesn't listen to you, you feel enraged." A third step, which is not always available to the therapist in the moment, is to *add the reasons* for the feeling: "When your daughter doesn't listen to you, you feel enraged *because* you want so much for her to love and respect you" or "because you feel she has no right to defy you." Young's (2006) abbreviation of this sequence is: "You feel (specific emotion) because (the facts of the situation that account for the emotion)." Practice reflecting feelings in a nonjudgmental way to encourage patients to more openly express their inner lives.

Identifying feelings is not always easy. An intervention that is often helpful when the therapist is not clear is to repeat the feeling word back to the patient with a questioning intonation, for example: "Irritated?" This asks the patient for more clarification on the particular feeling state. Reflecting back as a question the word you want to know more about is a useful tool in many situations. It is an open question that enables the patient to proceed in many directions but focuses his or her attention on the feeling. Beginning an inquiry in this more general way allows patients the freedom to reflect and then to follow their associations. This is especially important with trauma patients; for these patients, providing opportunities to be in control of their own process is part of their healing.

Culture, gender and family values often inhibit people from knowing, acknowledging or expressing their feelings. The ideas that men should not feel weak, that women shouldn't be angry, that we should not connect with ourselves, or that children shouldn't have ambivalent feelings about their parents are common in many cultures. Unlike the culture at large, however, the *zeitgeist* in the therapy room needs to contain the conviction that *whatever* the patient feels is OK and can be understood. Feelings are complex and often contradictory, so looking beyond the surface is necessary. Sometimes we must discern the feeling from subtle cues and by hearing what is said with the "third ear," as Theodore Reik described analytic listening.

We do not have to make perfect reflections. Rather, if our reflections are framed within a desire to more deeply understand our patients, they will usually sense our intentions and correct us when it is needed. Being able to model for patients an acceptance of our own fallibility, that we make mistakes, can be on the wrong track, misperceive or misunderstand the patient, or even to forget what a patient has told us is especially important for trauma patients. It demonstrates that we do not have to be perfect in order to be OK, or to value ourselves. Early trauma experiences are often formulated in the child's mind as shortcomings, failings or inadequacy. In the black and white mode of thinking that characterizes early childhood functioning, there may not be permission for mistakes and imperfection. Helping patients to see, in our interaction with ourselves as well as in how we relate to them, that we can accept and value our whole self provides a model for integration and can destabilize splitting.

When an intense level of traumatic memory is triggered, people are not just feeling something, not just remembering. They are *re-experiencing* the trauma as if it is happening right now. Emotionally, they are *convinced* that it is happening right now. Rational thought is trumped by the emotional trigger — emotion consistently holds the winning card. The combination of right-brain emotional conviction, that "this is the way things are," and left-brain deactivation leave the individual vulnerable to thoughts, feelings and fantasies that can be very far from reality.

CHAPTER 11

Listening for Defense

Fear is built into the structure of all living experience because it has adaptive value. We do not normally rush into burning buildings (unless we are firefighters) or move closer to snarling dogs or hissing snakes. Avoidance of these situations is adaptive and automatic; it keeps us out of harm's way. But not all avoidance is adaptive. Avoidance has multiple determinants and too much avoidance sets us up for problems in life.

Freud recognized early on that we seek to avoid pain and move toward pleasure. As with all living things, people seek to grow and preserve a sense of well-being. We work hard and sometimes are willing to pay a very high price (such as loss of self), for what feels like safety or emotional harmony. One of the ways we help ourselves to deal with discomfort, pain and trauma is through the development of defenses. Defenses help us to function in the face of threatening interactions, feelings, thoughts and fantasies.

We have explored the fundamental activities of listening for content and feeling. Our focus now will be on how we can listen for defense in order to uncover the traces of childhood organization and underlying mental processes. Learning to hear in this way, learning to identify and explore defensive activity, offers us an opportunity to examine issues patients push away, thereby making the treatment more effective.

Defense is, at its core, a type of avoidance, a moving away from threatening experience, an effort to make ourselves feel better. Therapists understand that the expectation of this type of painful experience is determined by many factors: early interactions with others, anticipation of negative interactions, fantasies about guilt, shame, punishment and early losses. Defense is part of the child's strategy for dealing with experience that can't be assimilated, a creative, generally unconscious way of relating to self and others that makes the child feel safer, protected, or more in control. Because defense is part of a childhood solution (in addition to being, at times, part of the problem), it is not something we seek to wrest from the patient. Defense in general is an ongoing organizational process in which the patient is profoundly invested. In relating to patients, this investment needs to be respected and *valued* for the way in which it has protected the patient's core self.

Even as we need to be mindful of the investments the patient has in defense and the importance of not attempting to rid patients of their defenses, we also need to keep ourselves (and sometimes our patients) aware of the power and perniciousness of avoidance. Avoidance almost instantaneously makes us feel better and is very compelling for that reason. Avoiding what disturbs us creates immediate physical, biological and psychological relief. Those who have experienced traumatizing childhood adversity often use avoidance as a matter of course, having learned at a very early age that there is an action they can take to make themselves feel better. At times, patients need psychoeducation to alert them to the dangers of avoidance, how its use can be a significantly rewarding experience, leading to increased avoidance and sometimes to panic attacks. Avoidance, especially in the mind of a cognitively immature child, stimulates the idea of being able to control a dangerously painful experience, generating secondary gains in addition to the immediate physical and emotional relief that follows from avoidant behavior. For many patients with a trauma history, avoidance is second nature and was perhaps one of the only things that they could actively do to protect themselves. Psychologically, however, avoiding what we fear reinforces the idea that there is something to be afraid of, rather than being able to assess the threat from a more balanced state. Avoidance therefore sustains our fears rather than giving us exposure to corrective experience. Although avoidance at first may seem like proactive engagement, often it leaves the sufferer with an increased sense of helplessness, a conviction that they are, indeed, living in the dangerous world of their fantasies. Psychologically, avoidance reinforces our specific ideas of dangerousness, thereby increasing our tendencies to avoid, creating a self-perpetuating cycle.

While therapist and patient need to be aware of the ways in which avoidance can exacerbate the patient's anxiety, when working with those who have a history of complex developmental trauma, we also need to be aware that the decision to confront anxiety, or not to use avoidant measures, is one that only patients can make. Facing down the terror one experienced as a child is a very difficult and courageous thing to do, and it must be done in the patient's own time. The therapist can encourage the patient to be aware that avoidance can make things worse and rejoice with the patient when they are able to stand their ground and risk not instituting avoidant behavior, but readiness to take these steps is always in the patient's hands. Only the patient can know the forces at work in these situations.

Our aim in working with defenses is to collaborate with the patient to explore them, to help the patient examine and understand the internal logic of their developmental strategies. We do not try to "overcome" the patient's defenses, for that would be structuring an authoritarian position into the therapeutic situation (Adler and Bachant, 1998). Our goal is not to rid patients of these defenses, because only the patient can make those decisions, often on a moment to moment basis. Rather, we seek to examine and explore, in short, to analyze these processes, together. By doing this we develop understanding. We uncover the vital ideas, beliefs, fantasies and attachments that keep these defenses in place. The patient's relationship to defensive processing begins to change as we work on examining what goes on when defensive processes are initiated. If explored in a context of safety and compassion, the patient's inner world can expand to include the uncovering of memories, thoughts, connections and emotions. Instead of blind adherence to emotionally dictated impulses that drowns out other voices, we make room for other inner voices. Defenses are automatic, triggered processes, brought into action when the patient senses an imminent danger. Analyzing these processes enables them to be integrated into the patient's self-understanding. Working with defensive processes gives us a road map into unexplored territories.

In common parlance we often hear that a person is self-sabotaging. By this label we are to understand that they tend to repeat the same action, even though it gets them into trouble time and again. A patient continually pursues women who are unavailable to him. Another cannot stop pushing people away with caustic comments. A third doesn't allow himself to finish work that would enhance his position in the world and his feelings about himself. We do a disservice to the process if we simply label these as self-sabotaging people. In these instances, multiple dynamics are at work to keep long-standing childhood strategies in place. Our job as therapists is to interest patients in exploring the many factors that tie them to patterns of behavior that bring them into conflict with themselves and others. Most often, these self-sabotaging patterns are rooted in unconscious, automatic, early defenses. For example, a boy may psychologically castrate himself in the face of powerful men as a way to demonstrate to the inner, abusive father of his childhood that he is out of the competition—he is no threat. Early defensive maneuvers helped children to feel safe. They were useful at the time and, in some important sense, they worked. There is a proactive aspect in the process of developing a defense (even a defense that is "self-sabotaging") that we can recognize and acknowledge. Understanding and appreciating children's survival instincts and their essential creativity in developing these defenses allows patients to have an ally in the process of changing these ways of approaching life. It helps patients see that even as very little children, they were proactively working to solve their problems in living.

How do we see and hear defense at work? Again, free association comes to our aid. We learn to listen not only to content, but to process; to not only to what the patient is saying, but what the patient is doing; not only to what the patient is doing but what he or she is not doing. An interruption in the flow of the patient's associations is often the first sign that defensive processes have been called into action. An ordinary conversation would let this go and wait for the person to resume talking. Therapy, however, is not an ordinary interaction. It is a special interaction with special rules and a unique framework (e.g., the freedom and obligation to say everything that comes to mind, and an acknowledgement that the interaction will be more focused on one of the participants than the other). And so, when the patient pauses or becomes silent, it can be appropriate for the therapist to inquire "What was going on when you paused after acknowledging that your friend disrespected you?" Instead of continuing to talk about the content (which is fully conscious and can wait), the therapist asks the patient to expand on something the patient revealed through his action of hesitating. When we notice the interruption in the flow of the patient's associations, we are letting patients know that we care about them and are genuinely interested in everything that they experience. We are also giving them an opportunity to direct their attention to what their hesitation was about—to turn the mind's eye to the process of moving away from something painful. This enables us to get to the core of the patients' fears and fantasies much faster than if we followed the content alone.

> Susan came into therapy in a crisis. She had found the love of her life but to her surprise, her love was another woman. She was brought up in a conservative and religious family. Prior to this she had not had these feelings about, or relationships with, women. Susan was disturbed and felt very isolated and alone. Typically, when she came in for her session, she sat on the couch opposite my chair and kept her arms folded across her chest, informing me that she had nothing to say. Often, she would begin the session saying, "I got nothing!"—demonstrating her deep conflict about entering the process (bringing herself to the session but cutting off any possibility of connecting with what was going on inside her). I am not sure how conscious I was at the time that her disconnection in the sessions was an

enactment of her experience relating to herself and others, including me. But I could clearly see that she had her guard up. Physically and verbally she demonstrated that although she would drag herself to therapy, she wasn't having any of it. Her defenses were up.

I began not by challenging the "nothing" she had to say, but by helping her to be curious about the kind of nothing she was experiencing today. Did it have an empty quality, a defiant one or something else? My nonjudgmental curiosity and interest in her experience helped us to see that just naming her feelings was challenging. Susan had cut herself off so profoundly from her own experience that knowing what she was feeling was often out of reach. With her arms still crossed during every session, we worked on identifying, elaborating and refining her understanding of her own experience, primarily from the starting point of her having nothing to say. As she began to feel safer, we began to connect. But still, Susan made clear in her posture toward me (arms still folded across her chest in every session) that she needed to ward off "this therapy thing." We took seriously her mode of relating to me and to herself, exploring and examining the thoughts and feelings in the room. Gradually, we became aware that in addition to having only a rudimentary awareness of her own experience, Susan's mode of relating was profoundly judgmental. Either I was talking "psychobabble" or she was contemptuous of her own experience or of my inquiries. My openness to hearing about the disdain she had for the therapy process, me, or herself, enabled her to gradually connect with me and parts of herself that she couldn't bear to see or feel. Susan's difficulty beginning the sessions and her posture throughout the sessions communicated the pervasive judging that was a part of her difficulty connecting with what was inside her. It took quite a long time, more than eight months, for Susan to trust me and the process enough to be able to be in a session without her arms defensively folded across her chest.

Another situation that comes up frequently in therapy is noticing that as patients are talking, emotions rise to the surface: patients will tear up, their mouths may quiver, their fists may clench. Commonly, the patient does not comment on these expressions of feeling, often swallowing the feeling or closing the gate on what was emerging. This is a process that deserves therapeutic attention: observing that an emotion that begins to emerge is followed by a defense. This process, of having emotions seep through is a vital aspect of how patients relate to themselves. One patient described it as a 'seeping through like water under a door, only to rush toward damming it up.' Helping patients to identify and observe this process by asking them to notice *"What just happened?"* engages patients in collaboration, so that they are looking at what just happened, while we are working together on figuring it out. Pointing the patient's attention to these moments helps patients to observe and reflect on their inner processes, rather than simply recounting them intellectually or being ensnared in the emotional current of their experience. In this way, we help patients to better understand what drives their experience while we work together on creating observing ego functions. Traumatized patients especially require the coming together of being able to access their terrors in the context of staying connected with the centered part of themselves. The more we help patients to notice their experience from a calm and compassionate perspective, the more they can apply observing ego functions on their own.

Listening for, identifying and hearing defensive function-ing, rather than interpreting defense, is our focus here. The vast majority of what we do with patients involves listening, making observations and encouraging patients to reflect on their own experience. These modes of relating keep us with the patient. Often our listening involves simply noticing an interruption in the flow of associations or a bodily expression of a feeling and asking the patient, "What just happened there?" Sometimes we can make a simple observation such as, "I noticed that you were tearing up as you spoke about your father." We do not have to have a complete understanding before we inquire. In fact, we inquire because we have questions and want to understand more. We listen for the footprints of latent content with our eyes as well as our ears, in the small, often bodily actions that are a part of the patient's expression. Hesitations, pauses, tone of voice, bodily expressions of feeling, misspoken words can all point to underlying fantasies, feelings and issues that we can bring to the center of therapeutic attention.

> Very early in her life, when she was 18 months old, Vita's world was forever changed by the birth of a baby brother. The little boy was born with a collapsed lung and needed special attention. Vita's position radically changed. Vita of course, does not explicitly remember what she experienced at so young an age, but somewhere inside her she knows how she felt: helpless, humiliated and heartbroken. These are the words she uses when talking about competing with her male colleagues at work, describing her work life with the same hopeless feelings that dominated her childhood.

In this chapter, we have talked about the way that anything—a feeling, a fantasy, a mode of relating, can be used to carry defensive functions.

What Vita and I reconstructed in a recent session, (primarily by noticing how she was relating to me in the transference with a hopeless, helpless demeanor), was that she must have looked at all the attention her baby brother was getting and decided (not consciously, of course) that if she too were helpless, she might be able to get back some of the love she had lost.

We see here a powerful feeling state that is being used defensively—a feeling of helplessness has become infused with the idea that if she looks, feels and acts helpless, like her baby brother was, she has a chance to get back the love that she lost as a little girl.

In one session we were able to identify that the feeling which emerged in our session was very similar to what she experiences with her male colleagues at work. Vita came to her next session close to tears. Three of her colleagues had not responded to her email requests. *"It's heartbreaking!"* She continued, saying that if she were someone else, they would have responded, but her situation was hopeless.

Our prior session had helped me to better understand how Vita's helplessness was an enactment of her early defensive strategy, something to explore, not to gratify. Looking back on previous sessions, I think I had been engaged in a transference enactment of a childhood fantasy with her in which I responded to her feeling of helplessness with caring concern and empathic responsiveness. Now I was seeing Vita's feeling of helplessness differently, more as a defense that needed to be examined than a feeling that needed to be supported.

I said to Vita, *"I understand that your situation at work is difficult and disappointing, even discouraging, but heartbreaking is an interesting word to use here."* Vita's word choice allowed us to see clearly that the experience of being heartbroken belonged to a much earlier time in her life. With this understanding, Vita had started to take in the idea that the feeling of helplessness was useful to her—helplessness gave her standing that she felt she lacked.

I would like to say that after we identified this defense everything got better. It did not. It took time for Vita to turn the corner. Defense is woven into the fabric of the person's sense of self. Unraveling it takes time and active struggling. In addition, it takes changing the patient's relationship to the part of herself that developed this defense in the first place. Vita understands much more about her impulse to make herself feel helpless. We are continuing to work on this aspect of her intrapsychic functioning. But more prominent now is the lack of compassion she feels toward that little two-year-old girl who had to figure out some way to get her parents back. All by herself, as a tiny little girl, Vita came up with the idea that making herself feel and act helpless, to be more like her baby brother, would get her what she so desperately needed. Even though this defense makes her feel very bad in the present, when she was a child it helped. Finding a way to get what she needed was a proactive, creative solution to an insurmountable emotional problem. So, as a child in this situation, Vita was far from helpless. She was actively solving the biggest problem in her life—and doing it with the limited resources of a two-year-old! Helping Vita see and identify with this proactive and determined part of herself provides a counterweight to the part of herself she sees as helpless.

I am going to end with a word about defense and resistance. Leo Rangell (1983) succinctly described resistance as a "defense against insight." We need to understand that resistance is an inevitable part of every therapeutic process from the very beginning of treatment. Therapy asks a lot from patients. In addition to looking inward, allowing oneself to see painful feelings, thoughts and fantasies, we are encouraging patients to change their fundamental psychic equilibrium. This is a monumental, and for most people, forbidding task. As Adler and I commented, resistance carries the "desperate effort to hold onto a fundamental orientation that makes sense of and stabilizes one's experience of the world. This orientation feels both desperately needed and painful to discard . . . . Analysis of resistance immerses us in powerful issues of attachment and separation, loss and integration, safety and avoidance" (1998, p. 106).

These issues are present from the beginning of the treatment and often manifest themselves in ideas about not being able to afford therapy, not being able to arrange a suitable time to meet, and any of a host of other "reality" based ideas that serve the patient's desire to escape the dangers of change. When dealing with the defense against insight, it is best not to engage patients in a power struggle that enacts the idea that we know better, that we know *what is really going on*. That strategy does not work. Rather, we can use patients' concerns as a way of exploring their conflicts, fantasies and ambivalence. To do this, an empathic acknowledgement of where patients are coming from is useful: "Yes, I realize that treatment is costly, and you may not be able to afford it right now. But it would be useful to understand what other factors may be at play. Remember, everything you think and feel, especially about your treatment, our relationship, even just vague anxieties will enable us to understand this situation as completely as possible." Communicating to patients that multiple factors are always involved, and that examining these factors will enable them to make the best decision for themselves often clears the path for further exploration. Examining the patient's fears, associations and thoughts about the therapist often, but not always, enables the patient to continue in treatment. Sometimes, however, we need to be prepared to understand that readiness for treatment may take more time, or that we are not the patient's cup of tea. Truly appreciating the daunting nature of the task that patients sign up for when they begin therapy enables us to respect their decision, whatever it may be.

CHAPTER 12

Listening for Transference/ Countertransference

We listen for transference and countertransference in the patterns of relating that are revealed in the therapy relationship. Part of the reason why we structure the therapeutic situation as we do, focused primarily on the patient with the therapist remaining more opaque, is to facilitate the emergence of fantasies and unconscious patterns of relating that can then be brought to the center of therapeutic attention. This is useful because our brains naturally tend to fill in the blanks when we are confronted with situations that are unclear (Cozolino, 2002). The therapist's relative opaqueness provides the patient with a living Rorschach onto which early patterns of relating can be projected, giving us clues about how unconscious processes are organized. Leaving room to reflect (a crucial element), within a therapeutic structure that provides some ambiguity about the therapist, encourages transference phenomena to emerge and become a more visible part of the therapeutic interaction. Of course, who the therapist is will be reflected in everything he or she does. Patients are very good at picking up the subtlest of cues. The point here is that the asymmetry of the structure of the therapeutic situation leaves room for ambiguity. This is technically useful. It enables us to better listen for and see our patient's transferential activity.

In order to listen for transference, however, we first need to know what we are looking for. When therapists speak about transference, they are referring to the organizing activity of childhood wishes, emotions, and relational configurations that have different levels of integration with the evolving self. As mentioned earlier, transference is relatedness embodied. It is relatedness that is revived, expressed and symbolized in the therapeutic interaction. We transfer the modes of relating to the world we apprehended as children onto an organization of the present (Adler and Bachant, 1998). Relatedness to our bodies and our significant others is the first territory we explore as children. Transference activity, mediated through fantasy and the body, actualizes the influence of past relatedness in the present. Some aspects of transference activity are seamlessly integrated into our sense of self, informing, for example, our identifications, what we do and who we love. Although life choices are always multidetermined, the quality and history of our relatedness to self and others organize the path of our life's journey. Healthy, integrated, less conflicted transference configurations are generally adaptive; they serve the overall needs of the person. Identification with the kindness of one's father or the authority of one's mother are examples of what might be adaptive transference activity that is generally well integrated into the person's sense of self.

Other aspects of transference, because they developed in traumatic relationships or situations characterized by higher levels of conflict, defense and painful affects, are less integrated into core self functioning and tend to be more isolated and split off. This type of transference activity is more rigidly tied to archaic feelings and fantasies and is less integrated into one's central sense of self.

> Anna's choice to become a physician was highly influenced by the helplessness she felt as little girl felt when she was not able to save her father who died next to her in a car accident. This choice was adaptive for Anna in many ways and it suited her. It helped her to feel more in control of life-threatening situations. Anna's past haunted her, however, in her presenting symptom: she would become paralyzed with panic every time one of her patients took a turn for the worse. Early transferential fears and fantasies were getting triggered from archaic mental processing. The task of trying to save her patients, whose lives were, in fact, endangered became imbued with imperative childhood wishes and fears around saving her father. Anna needed to be able to differentiate the childhood helplessness she felt in the face of her father's car accident from her present situation where her patients were in danger.

Another example of less integrated, less adaptive transference activity: Peter's choice of a life partner was strongly influenced by an unmet need to be loved and accepted by a narcissistic mother, necessitating a maladaptive, narcissistic object choice in order to stand in for the desire to gain this particular kind of mother's love in fantasy. In this situation, only a narcissistic woman fills the bill. We can listen for and examine with the patient these off-target transference manifestations, interactions that reveal intense transference triggering but are a step removed from being experienced directly between the therapeutic collaborators. Listening for the patterns of relating that characterize this patient's interactions with others enables us to better identify when the transference wishes and fears are directly expressed in the therapeutic process. Listening for transference involves being alert to patterns of relating that come to pervade interactions with others as well as relatedness with the self.

> Vita comes to her session with two exciting job possibilities. Before this, she had been looking fruitlessly for eight months. She quickly transitions away from her excitement and toward feeling hopeless and helpless about selling herself, triggered by the dilemma of having to give her elevator pitch to 30 asset managers. She is soon in tears, comparing herself with others and feeling that she falls appallingly short. I am struck both by my impatience with her insistence on relating to herself as inadequate and by my desire to help her out of her misery. I also note her quick conversion of excitement into despair. Is my countertransferential fantasy of taking care of her something that she has been unconsciously reading and enacting with me? Is there a way that she "prefers" the despair because it brings me closer to her? Is she enacting a fantasy in which I punish her for her imaginary wrongdoing? I choose to ask her to notice the process of her movement from excitement to despair. Vita doesn't want any part of this. Instead she continues with the theme of doing things wrong: how she spent hours and hours this weekend digesting an article about the issues involved when foreign banks sell derivatives in the US when she should have been networking or working on getting more meetings. I notice again that she seems to prefer talking to me about what she is doing

wrong to engaging her excitement with me and in herself. I also connect with an awareness of how punishing herself, her self-castigating, is so easily evoked. I acknowledge to myself that I am certainly feeling more impatient with this pattern. I am not sure on which theme I should focus: the self-punishment or the disconnection from her own excitement. Perhaps they are related. Remembering a discussion in a recent session of how her sexual desire has been radically curtailed in her marriage, I ask her if staying with the excitement makes her anxious. Vita pauses and seems noticeably uncomfortable.

"I don't want to get excited because I know that I will be disappointed."

"Focusing on what you are doing wrong seems very important to you. We need to understand why it overrides allowing yourself to connect with your own excitement."

"I don't want to feel miserable all the time! I just know that I can't do it right. I'm just not good enough." Vita returns again to the theme that we have identified and talked about from many angles: the feeling of helplessness and hopelessness that she experienced at a very young age when she "lost" her mother to the birth of three siblings in quick succession and "failed" at making things better. I note to myself that although she seems to be developing an understanding of this patterning, something is keeping her tied to it. I wonder if the gratification of being able to obtain my solicitude outweighs the misery she has to endure in order to connect with me. The theme of punishing remains in a corner of my mind. Her resistance to take in and integrate our work on this aspect of her functioning has a powerful payoff: the enactment of a transferential fantasy of finally being able to get her mother's attention even if it comes at a cost of terrible suffering.

"Maybe being able to get my solicitude is more important than the suffering you have to go through to get it."

"Are you saying that I'm making myself miserable in order to connect with you?"

"I think it's something we need to consider. I have noticed that even though we have talked about this pattern from many angles, it is very easy for you to slip into it. Although there is an automaticity to this experience, other things may be involved. Feeling this way makes you so miserable. There may be an even greater payoff that keeps you tied to this pattern."

"I see what you are talking about. But it feels so real."

"It was real. It was your powerfully felt reality when you were a three-year-old struggling with losing your mother and not understanding why you "failed" to get her back. Maybe getting her back through our relationship trumps everything else."

A lot is going on in this snippet of our work. Vita is demonstrating resistance to integrating, preferring (on some level) instead to enact a fantasy of finally getting the emotional concern of her mother even though she has to pay the price of making herself miserable in order to do it. Another resistance is in play although we did not deal with it in this session—the desire to punish herself for her own failure to be good enough to get her mother back. My countertransferential impatience with her passionate insistence on berating herself points to an enactment in which Vita still blames herself for the loss of her mother and punishes herself for her failing. I can sense the movement here from an intrapsychic enactment (how she is relating to herself) to an interpersonal one (my impatience, bordering on irritation). Her anxiety about allowing herself to be excited, about the job possibilities, with her husband, or with me are interwoven in this process. At least three dimensions of resistance are operative: enacting and through it gratifying a fantasy of getting her mother's love through our relationship; punishing herself for her imagined childhood failure to get her mother back and keeping herself warded off from the anxieties aroused by relating through gratifying engagement in the present. All these dimensions are represented in our transference/countertransference process.

We must keep in mind that transference activity, fueled by fantasy, and by very early learning and years of neural priming is ubiquitous. Transference infuses all experience. So, when listening for transference, we do not have to look far. Transference activity is present in how patients relate to their friends, their lovers, their work, their bosses, their therapists, their pets, their fears and their choices about virtually everything that is important. Two types of transference activity claim special attention in therapy: transference activity in relation to the therapist and transference activity in relation to the self. How patients organize their perception of and relation to the therapist is actively present from their first encounter. Patients also bring their transferentially based modes of relating with themselves into every session. In fact, how patients relate to themselves is also reflected in how they relate to the therapist. Listening for transference activity — *how* they are relating to the therapist and *how* they are relating to themselves — gives us a productive focus for listening.

Laurie's reaction to a moment of connection in our work together was often followed by a voice inside her that said, "All right, you've done enough here. You may as well leave." When I inquired about her impulse to leave, she told me that she felt like walking out of the room and even more, of ending the treatment. She said that anything good that happened between us just seemed like a "dead end." Although Laurie had used this phrase before, and I had probed for her associations to it, this time I had a fantasy of her dead ending herself, killing herself off. When I shared my fantasy with her, she immediately connected to the idea, saying that many times in her childhood she wished she were dead, or that she just didn't exist. This inquiry led to an exploration of her actively cutting herself off from thoughts and feelings that were too painful to bear, especially when she started to hope for more connectedness. A memory emerged of her yelling at herself in reference to her mother after a younger sister was born and the patient was taken from her mother and given to her critical grandmother for caretaking: "She's not coming back! She's not coming back!" she screamed at herself in rage. Anger moved in to be her prime mode of connecting, as relatedness through more tender feelings was much more frightening. The exchange between us allowed Laurie to connect with more compassion for the pain she endured as a child, as well as to understand herself as an active agent of what she was experiencing.

Just as listening carefully to what is happening at the beginning of the session is specially valued because it brings patients' immediate and often unconscious concerns to the fore, so listening to how patients begin the very first session will tell us a lot about their transference organization. Although our goal is to generate a collaborative mode of relating, we cannot abrogate the position of authority in which we find ourselves when doing therapy. That the patient is suffering and is coming to us for help is a primary organizer of the relationship, one that stimulates transferences to the therapist as an authority. Listening for the nature of the transference activity with which our patients relate to us from the very beginning can be a shortcut to deeper engagement.

> Jonathan came to his first session revealing that he had looked me up on the internet before coming for his appointment. "I checked you out on the internet. You are an expert and come well-recommended, so I hope you can help me. I have been struggling for a long time and now my business is starting to be affected. I am spread so thin that I can't do anything well. I've been in therapy before, but nothing seems to help."

Before Jonathan stepped foot in my office, he made clear that my being an authority was important to him. When we look at his initial communication, we see three references to ensuring that I could fulfill his need for an authority. This redoubling of an idea is something that we take notice of—it speaks with a louder voice than a simple mention, for example, of the fact that I came well-recommended. But Jonathan goes further in this initial communication, revealing an added dimension to his transferential activity. He tells me that no one and nothing has been able to help, revealing the deep sense of helplessness he brings to the therapist and to the process of relating to himself as well. Jonathan is not only deferring to the authority of the therapist. He is also letting me know how important it is to have such an authority, and that I fill the bill. How nice, I mused to myself, to be well thought of.

My countertransferential seduction had begun. I didn't think it quite consciously, but a fantasy of being the authority who could unlock the door of his suffering began to roll around in the recesses of my mind. The pull away from a collaborative mode of relating toward a more transference-directed authoritative one had started to surface. Along with his bid for a more directive mode of relating, Jonathan is communicating the helplessness he experiences in both self and other relating (other therapists have not been able to help him, and he has not been able to help himself). Jonathan longs for an authority to fix his problems but is also showing us through the transference that his own helplessness is an important part of the picture. Is his need for an authority connected with the helplessness he feels? Is the failure, and his reporting the failure, of his previous therapies enacted in this dynamic? Is keeping himself feeling helpless an important piece of his relationship to authority? Is thwarting the authority a part of this puzzle? Listening for transferential activity even at the very beginning of a treatment can give us a handle on how the patient organizes his life, and what areas need further exploration. How directly and how soon we will want to engage the understanding that emerges from this type of listening will vary with the situation.

Perhaps one of the most useful tools for grasping a patient's transference is training ourselves to monitor our own sensibilities as we speak with the patient. Our countertransferential pushes and pulls are often good indicators of what transference activity the patient may be experiencing: the feelings, fantasies, wishes and fears organized through early relating that are now stimulated by our interaction. If we feel deadness in the room, for example, it is worth pursuing the possibility that the patient may be cutting herself off. If we get irritated with a patient, we will want to think about the possibility that punishing or sadistic fantasies have been stimulated in our interaction. If we feel an impulse to mother the patient, we need to ask ourselves if the patient is positioning himself as a child in the relationship.

Transference/countertransferential activity can be thought of as existing on a spectrum of interaction (Lynch, Bachant and Richards, 1998) that converges in enactments, interactions between patient and therapist that take their relatedness to the level of *acting out* early experiences and internalized modes of relating. It is in enactments that the space between the patient and therapist comes alive in the treatment.

CHAPTER 13

Listening for Meaning

Meaning is at the core of how experience is apprehended. It is also at the center of how the mind is organized, and therefore at the nexus of defense, resistance, transference and the sense of what is good and bad. We have spoken about the centrality of feeling in understanding a patient's experience. According to Browning (2019) and contemporary neuropsychologists (Clyman, 1991; LeDoux, 1998; Ginot, 2015; Panksepp, 1997; Solms and Panksepp, 2012; Solms, 2013) affect, i.e., emotional experience is foundational. Emotional experience motivates learning, relatedness and cognition as well as forming the basis of our symbolic minds. Meaning is grounded in the way affect becomes uniquely organized for each person, incorporating symbolic thought that goes beyond linguistic marking. Browning comments that "the real import of a symbolic system of reference is its use in referring to *relationships* among objects and events," (emphasis added) enabling the development of logical categorization of entities at higher and higher levels of abstraction. Symbolic thinking also makes possible the analytic breakdown of objects and events into smaller and smaller units (Browning, 2019, p. 30). *Therapy involves not only pointing at specific aspects of experience but establishing meaningful connections between different levels of functioning.* Without the unifying thread of meaning, we cannot see the essence of our patient's experience in the world.

It cannot be stressed enough that *meaning is always uniquely individual*. We cannot speculate about the meaning an event carries for a group of people in general, even if they have experienced the same trauma. Meaning always has to be defined from an inner perspective. To different people, an earthquake can mean a punishment inflicted because of some wrongdoing, an opportunity to demonstrate strength or courage, a chance to help others, or a hundred other things. Finding the unique meaning a patient assigns to a given experience is often difficult, especially as the meanings of many experiences are determined by very early childhood events, wishes, fears and fantasies, many of which are outside conscious awareness. Meaning is intrinsic to how experience is represented. It is generally symbolic in nature. Often it must be cobbled together from symbolic resonance, reading between the lines, connotative and denotative associations, feelings, fantasies, and memories as well as transference/countertransference, resistance, and enactments. Meaning carries a person's innermost wishes and fears.

More than any discipline, psychoanalysis has devoted itself to examining, exploring and thinking about how meaning is created and expressed, hidden, enacted and organized in our relationships. The content of a communication is often only the top layer of what the person means. To obtain the fullest understanding of our patients, we need to be able to grasp not only the surface meaning of communication, but also the figurative, historical, symbolic and personal meaning that resides in the narrative. Many students have found distinguishing between the manifest and latent content of what the patient says to be especially helpful.

Freud first spoke of manifest and latent content in connection with understanding dreams, but he was not interested in deciphering dreams for their own sake. Rather, he wanted to develop a general psychology, an understanding of how the mind works. Generations of thinkers after Freud have used this distinction beyond dream work, to help give the therapist access to the unconscious processes that infuse all communication. In fact, we now know that the unconscious forces that make dream work so compelling pervade all aspects of a patient's communications. The unconscious is an "equal opportunity employer," using whatever is at hand to represent and carry the patient's dynamic issues. We do not have to wait for a dream to find the royal road to the unconscious. Our every act, thought, feeling, idea, fantasy and conflict is replete with meaning and unconscious manifestations. This understanding helps us to appreciate that *all* communication is grounded in the meaning it embodies.

The manifest content is the descriptive story of a patient's communication. The manifest content contains the narrative contents as well as mental images as they appear to the speaker. Staying with the patient in depth involves going beyond the manifest content—developing the ability to see the latent and symbolic content in the patient's manifest account. The dynamically skilled therapist listens for the underlying themes that motivate the sequence of associations. For example, Eric's communications typically involve a need to aggrandize himself, while Vincent's presentation often involves presenting himself as a victim. This underbelly of communication reflects the imprint of unconscious conflicts, fantasies, wishes and fears, known collectively as the latent content. Latent content can be ascertained from many aspects of the patient's speech: the word a patient picks to express a certain feeling; the particular free associations that emerge in the process; a tone that invades the communication whenever the patient talks about a specific topic; symbolic resonance; the particular sequencing of the patient's presentation, etc. Thinking about *how* the patient communicates in addition to *what* the patient communicates opens the door to exploring latent content.

We see latent content in a patient's actions when they pay us too much or too little for a session. Or when they disavow their experience ("I don't mean to be picky, but . . . ." or "I don't want to insult you, but . . ." or "Don't take this the wrong way, but . . ."). Or when their associations lead inevitably to a familiar theme, content or sequence. For example, one patient said in a session, "My sister and I are both riddled with competition but mine is more virulent." Her choice of the word virulent communicates the depth and potential lethality of her competitive strivings. At another time this patient, who was very anxious about allowing herself to stay with good feelings, came to her session remarking, "What a glorious spring day we are having in the middle of winter!" only to follow her comment with another that moved her from joyful appreciation to anxious anticipation: "But when you think about it, that it comes from climate change, it's really quite frightening." This is an example of hearing latent content in the sequencing of the patient's process. The sequencing reveals her uncomfortableness with staying with her own enjoyment.

Paradoxically, meaning is often both omnipresent and hidden. It needs to be unpacked from the patient's verbal and nonverbal communications, and from the transference/countertransference modes of relating to the therapist. The most important thing to understand about the meaning that a person gives to an experience is that it is inevitably tied to the history of that person's experience.

> Michael came to therapy because he had lost his job and it panicked him. Being a good provider was the driving force in his life and to not have a job was devastating. Married with a son, whom he adored but rarely saw because of his long work days, he was the primary provider for his family. I had the sense from the beginning that his panic had deeper roots. But Michael had little interest in talking about anything else. In fact, transferentially, I felt somewhat locked out of deeper connection with Michael. So consumed was he with regaining employment that nothing else seemed to matter.

> Michael lost his father to a long illness when he was six years old. Although he had a vague sense of fondness for his father, Michael's connection to his own emotional life was tenuous at best. He loved his wife and did not have relationships outside the home, but he was uncomfortable with closeness and had minimal interest in sex. He adored his son although he spent little time with him, and desperately wanted to spare him from experiencing any suffering. His primary passion was wrapped up in the idea of providing for his family, "giving my family what they need." His predominant fantasies involved many iterations of providing for his family financially so that they would not have to endure the losses and anxieties he experienced after his father's death. Becoming a good provider helped Michael feel secure. In his mind, it had the meaning of protecting him and them from the powerful emotional losses that invaded his life after his father's death.

When he lost his job, the insecurities of his early life erupted with a vengeance. Michael became obsessed with getting another job and spent all his time, including nights and weekends, engaged in the hunt for new employment. In the middle of all this, Michael's wife came to him and asked for a divorce.

We can understand Michael's obsession with being a good provider as a childhood strategy that helped protect himself from deeper emotional concerns: his anxieties rooted in feelings and fantasies about loss. My experience of being "locked out," pushed away from more authentic emotional engagement with Michael was a harbinger of how he was relating on an emotional level: pushing away emotional connection. Only the specter of losing his wife and family enabled Michael to bring himself to confront the emotional constriction he had developed after the trauma of his father's death. Early in Michael's life, fantasies of financial security had come to have the meaning of emotional security. His pursuit of financial security provided him with the illusion of protecting himself from the helpless, hopeless feelings of loss that so affected him as a child.

We must use caution when extracting evidence of unconscious dynamics. Thoughtfulness, tact and timing are essential considerations when working with latent content. A collaborative relationship that has the patient's growth and understanding at its center is essential. To be avoided is the type of "wild analysis" that characterized the early days of psychoanalysis, where considerations of tact and timing were not intrinsic aspects of the work. We must always be wary of impulses to use the treatment to gratify our own narcissistic impulses at the patient's expense. Patients in psychotherapy, like students of psychotherapy, need time and conscious examination to nurture the development of a collaborative foundation. This foundation enables patients and therapists to work together to uncover dynamic patterns and explore the tangled webs of latent processing that hold these patterns in place.

Reflections of Meaning

There are many kinds of reflections of meaning. I will illustrate one basic technique. In this formulation, the reflection of meaning takes essentially the same structure as reflections of feeling: Identify the feeling and add your sense of the reason for those feelings. For example, a reflection of *feeling* with Marsha, a patient who is struggling with her husband's increasing dementia would be:

"You feel hopeless because you can't get your husband to seek help for his growing dementia."

Reflections of meaning follow this structure but add the *meaning* behind the situation that accounts for the feeling.

"You feel hopeless because your husband's growing dementia makes you confront the fact that you are losing him."

The hopelessness this patient feels is empathically acknowledged with the feeling reflection, but it is deepened by the reflection of meaning. This first reflection of meaning can lead to others that continue to deepen the work because one meaning is not the end of the path to understanding. Meanings are often nested within each other like a set of Russian dolls (Richards, 2005). The reflection in this exchange is situated in the deep meaning of the patient's relationship with her husband. But her hopelessness about loss has other meanings that reside in and below her awareness of the current situation. Meaning pervades human experience. It is always there. Helping the patient to drill down to these deeper levels of meaning is something we will develop as we look at enactments and organization.

CHAPTER 14

Listening for Enactment

Enactments are modes of relating that embody our earliest emotional and defensive patterns. According to Ginot (2015), the repetition of these relational systems is an automatic, unconscious and inevitable aspect of "brain/mind" development. What becomes enacted between patient and therapist (and enacted in how the patient relates to self) are implicit emotional and relational patterns. Often, these patterns of relating were developed very early, before verbal memory and the left hemisphere developed. What is significant about these pre-verbal, right-brain dominated patterns of relating is that they are vulnerable to incorporating core emotionally-based fear reactions, thereby creating a negative bias. Emotionally driven, highly distorted representations of self and other, generated by immature, self-blaming "explanations" for painful situations are the hallmarks of enactments (Ginot, 2015; Gazzaniga, 2008; Schore, 2012). They are understood by some to be automatic, carrying an intense, usually negative, feeling tone, and conveying a sense of conviction that dominates experience. Ginot describes enactments as "mutually reactivated self-systems or entangled implicit relational schemas" that serve as a gateway to the patient's unconscious relational system (Ginot, 2015, p. 77). In other words, enactments are early modes of relating to self or others triggered intrapsychically (by different aspects of self relating) or interpersonally (by relating to another person). We also see enactments that merge intrapsychic and interpersonal functioning, as when intrapsychic fantasies are projected onto others. Enactments show us the patterns of relating to self and others that were organized very early in the patient's life. In order to obtain the most complete working through of the emotional activation, the gratifications that enactments carry in the present need to be identified and worked through in the ongoing therapeutic engagement.

The concept of enactments was developed first in terms of acting out between patient and therapist, often involving interactions that pulled the therapist out of the therapeutic frame. As therapists, we use our countertransferential awareness to awaken us to the processes that emotional activation has pulled us into unwittingly. We learn to pay attention even to passing thoughts and peripheral feelings as well as more developed mental processes. Enactments involve feelings in both participants that are automatic and emotionally compelling. They also have a lot to teach us about the nature of the patient's relatedness.

We need to understand that enactments *may or may not* involve the therapist directly. *Enactments, like transference, resistance and defense, are all around us; they are representations of how our minds organize and process the world.* Enactments are especially available for therapeutic work in *how patients relate to themselves*. Patients enact their relatedness to others in how they relate to themselves.

Identifying Enactments—With Others and with Self

Enactments *always* involve emotional activation. This triggering can be as loud as a torrent of rage or as quiet as a ripple in a calm pool. It is useful to differentiate the two. A hard trigger involves an intensely felt de-centering of the patient's emotional experience. Patients feel this intense emotional activation in their bodies. Unless dissociation is marked, they know they are not in their normal state. They may not be able to control the arousal, but they know it is happening. This is what I call a hard trigger. Hard triggers often involve archaic fantasies and feelings based in childhood assessment of experience. Because these experiences have been split off, not integrated into the patient's sense of self, they tend to be intense, automatic and emotionally loaded. If they developed very early, they may also have a negative bias—towards self-hatred, or self-blame or, for example, an unreasonable expectation that no one can be trusted.

What can be more difficult for therapist and patient to identify is the soft trigger, the experience of being triggered when it is woven into the fabric of the patient's sense of self, when it is part of the air they breathe (Howell 2005). This manifestation of an early, archaic enactment fits seamlessly into the patient's sense of self and is therefore difficult to identify as a trigger.

Let's return to the reflection of meaning with Marsha, the patient whose husband was developing dementia:

"You feel hopeless because your husband's growing dementia makes you confront the fact that you are losing him."

When this reflection was made, the patient started to sob uncontrollably. Although Marsha was connecting to the reality of her current loss, the quality of her reaction indicated that *beyond* the present-day sadness of her loss, she was also being emotionally triggered. Confronting the loss of her husband *is* a significant loss. But the intensity and quality of her sobbing were of a different order. They indicated to me that underneath the loss of her spouse were other, even more powerful losses that were activated by her *associations* to the present loss. This patient had a mother who acted out her anger at her by disconnecting from the patient emotionally when she was very young. One way of many ways the mother would enact her own anger was by keeping silence. Marsha remembered interminable days while her mother kept silent. It is a very difficult thing to lose a spouse that you love and have been with for many years. It is intolerable to lose a parent when you are a little child. The possibility that this patient was injecting her archaic fears of being emotionally abandoned as a child into her present experience needed to be considered. Sensing the presence of an intrapsychic enactment, after she had ample time to connect with her feelings of loss, I commented:

"I wonder if your fear of losing your husband has triggered all the times you felt so helplessly abandoned by your mother when she would get mad at you."

In this intervention, I identified the feeling and connected it to the re-enactment, the re-emergence of early feelings she experienced when her mother emotionally disconnected from her. I could make this connection because the effects of her childhood developmental trauma had been an ongoing topic of our work together. This very early kind of emotional arousal needs to be clarified to the patient for what it is: an emotionally driven, highly distorted image of self/other generated by immature, self-blaming thinking. Learning how to identify the quality of the emotion and having openness to the idea that archaic intrapsychic enactments may be involved can help the therapist to go beyond interpretations of meaning. The timing and approach we use are critical and can require waiting minutes or even days before readiness is achieved. In this case, waiting until Marsha had returned to a more integrated state was necessary in order to continue exploring her experience. Identifying the triggering process after she had time to come back to her normal self state enabled her to differentiate the experience of losing her husband from that of being a helpless and terrified child. It is hard enough to lose a spouse without infusing that loss with the feelings of hopelessness and helplessness she had *as a child*.

The infusion of childhood-derived meaning into present day patterns of living renders understandable behaviors that initially seem inexplicable. Helping patients see the meaning and organization they are expressing in their feelings, actions and behaviors enables them to embrace themselves and to pro-actively engage their now self-defeating patterns in a way that is not possible without grasping underlying meaning.

Susan grew up in a home with a domineering but lov-ing father who was more connected to his sons than to his daughters. The father was very high functioning and demanded a high level of performance from his chil-dren. The patient was often ridiculed for being sensi-tive—"Sensitive Susan" was a nickname that disparaged her emotional relatedness. Susan coped with these issues by identifying with her father's aggression and demands, becoming a good child, and thinking always of others at the cost of cutting off her emotional life. In her adolescence, Susan began to rebel against her father by binge eating. She would sneak the food she wanted, thereby satisfying her desire to acknowledge her inner cravings, to feel free of her father's demands, and to give herself relief from the expe-rience of being controlled. She developed the minimally conscious idea that comfort and the ability to connect with herself and to make herself feel good were to be found in the action of eating whatever she wanted, despite her father's displeasure. But there is more to this enactment. Binge eating resulted in the patient gaining weight, which made her very unhappy. Her bad feelings about disobeying her father's demands (as well as her own wishes to be a normal weight) left Susan feeling depressed, mortified, and helpless. In addition to asserting her independence, Susan's enactment of binge eating gratified needs to be punished by her father (and herself) for daring to think and act with independence. Comforting and connecting with herself was allowed only if she simultaneously punished herself for these desires. Sometimes this enactment would be directly acted out in the therapeutic relationship as the patient would talk about the pints of ice cream she was going to have after the session, trying to engage the therapist in taking her father's directive role. Most times, however, it was enacted in how she related to herself, repeating the cycle of taking care of herself, gratifying inner cravings, *but only* if punishment for her independence, for connecting to her own desires was involved.

In addition to hard and soft triggers, when thinking about enactments it is also helpful to ask whether the enactment represents primarily an intrapsychic or interpersonal mode of relating. These two categories are not mutually exclusive though it is useful to talk about them separately. When I speak about an intrapsychic enactment, I am referring to an automated, emotionally-driven, less conscious mode of relating to the self. Interpersonal enactments involve actions that are anticipated, developed or taken within the therapeutic relationship or with others. We must keep in mind that interpersonal enactments are often projections or representations of intrapsychic processing, how one relates to self. Enactments are based on unconscious early modes of relating that are now automatic. As such, interactions between intimate others (husbands and wives, parents and children, siblings, etc.) are particularly vulnerable to the emergence of enactments. In the treatment situation, the therapist becomes an intimate other, a target for the longings, fears and fantasies that organize experience. Below is an example of an enactment that occurred with the therapist which had both interpersonal and intrapsychic dimensions.

> Mia was 32-years-old when she came to me for treatment. The child of two professionals, she had had an upper middle-class childhood. Her presenting problem was that she had concerns about ending her marriage to a man with whom she felt little connection. Initially, our sessions were quite straightforward, although I did notice that she looked warily at me and manifested a need to be in control. I also noticed some emotionality when she described her parents. but she avoided answering direct questions about this. I wasn't sure what the arousal was related to and, because it was at the very beginning of our work together, decided to respect her sequence and give her more time to open up. We worked together for two and a half months. I thought the treatment was going well. We were getting to some of her core issues and developing a good working alliance.
>
> Then, quite suddenly, she came to her session with tears in her eyes. The first thing she said was that she had to stop coming. She couldn't do this anymore. She became visibly upset and started crying but couldn't talk. I was flummoxed. I didn't understand what had happened.

What *was* happening. Inwardly, I reflected on our last few sessions to see if there was something I did or said that was distressing to Mia. Remembering her need for control, I wondered if I had pushed her too hard. I had no idea what was going on, but I had a feeling that I had done something wrong. When I could not connect to anything, I asked about this directly: "Have I done or said something that has stimulated these feelings?" She responded, *"No, no. It isn't you. It's just that it's been two and a half months and I just have to stop."* I thought about this for a few moments. Her tears subsided somewhat and because there was nothing else to grab hold of, I asked, *"What about two and a half? . . . What comes to mind about two and a half?"* At this point she broke down sobbing. After considerable time, she calmed down a little and told me in barely a whisper, *"When I was two and a half, I stopped speaking. I had been very verbal till then, but I didn't talk at all after that until I was four years old."* I don't remember exactly what I said—my recollection is that I didn't want to say much but wanted to let her know I wanted to hear what she needed to tell me. Her action of wanting to leave the treatment was a powerful statement in itself that we needed to decipher. It suggested that her intrapsychic mode of dealing with the problem was to move away from it. Certainly, her actions in the session made me wonder if something had happened when she had stopped speaking when she was two and a half years old.

I did ask Mia if there was *anything* she remembered from that time. She then told me that she remembered having a recurrent nightmare throughout her childhood. She would be in bed and she would see a child's drawing in red crayon of a man's face. The picture would get closer and closer, and closer, until it was in her face and throbbing with intensity. She sobbed more. Finally, she said *"I think my father molested me."*

Mia did not leave treatment, and although she did not immediately remember the details of her sexual abuse, dreams and memories gradually emerged. Now I understood her wariness and need for control. Together we worked on piecing together her history as well as how she related to the acknowledgement of her warded-off experience. We also spoke about how she wanted to deal with her parents. Although this enactment of her experience took me by surprise, it did generate in me feelings that I had somehow harmed her, that I had somehow done something wrong. My respect for her experience and my nonjudgmental curiosity to understand the trigger for her intense reaction enabled me to continue to explore this intense and emotionally loaded situation.

This enactment occurred within the interpersonal sphere of the therapeutic relationship but was weighted toward the place on the spectrum of interaction (Lynch, Bachant and Richards, 1998) that primarily involves the patient acting out her experience in the immediacy of the therapy encounter. In other situations, the therapist more fully embraces the enactment process and contributes to an ongoing engagement that reenacts an important pattern of relating.

Vita entered the office lugging the computer she had purchased about six weeks ago after a leak from the apartment above had damaged her old one. Virtually every time she came in for her twice weekly sessions she complained about her shoulder, her back, her arms . . . how much they were hurting her. Understanding that everything a patient brings into the treatment room has significance, even if it is outside the usual boundaries of the session, a few sessions ago I had observed that this new computer really seemed to be hurting her. I was inviting her to look at this ongoing pattern of relating to herself. Vita had much more important things to talk about and brushed off my interest with a reassuring smile and a quick, *"Oh, it's really fine."* This time, however, I found myself enacting an impulse that I did not foresee and was not able to constrain. *"Vita!" I exclaimed with an exasperated tone. Why don't you get yourself a different computer! This has been going on for a long time!"* While Vita was justifying her behavior—the insurance paid for this one, and she had wanted one with a bigger screen and with more bells and whistles, and it really wasn't so bad, etc., etc. I was noticing the impulsiveness of my action in how quickly and decisively I had intervened. What was going on? I wasn't sure. But my action was certainly emotionally loaded, and although phrased as a question, it was much more a command. Not my usual mode of relating. Something was being enacted between us, but I wasn't sure what it was. Was I impatient with her masochism and starting to play the sadist in an unconscious drama between us? Was I trying to protect her? Was I punishing her for not taking care of herself? All of the above? Something else? I took a couple of deep breaths to calm myself and began to listen, both to her and to myself.

As I was listening to Vita, I became aware that the thread that ran through her associations involved not only not taking care of herself but also punishing herself. She spoke about her struggles over the weekend, putting off what she wanted to do, and then being angry at herself for her choices. A fantasy of helplessness intruded into my thoughts about her. Was she demonstrating to me how poorly she took care of herself to communicate her desire for me to help her? Was making herself helpless (over the weekend and with her choice of computer), a price she was willing to pay, in order to call out for my ministrations? Although we did not get to fully explore these questions until several sessions later, my countertransferentially based enactment with her alerted us to a process that she couldn't talk about but that she desired to bring into the treatment. It was the beginning of an exploration of the payoffs involved in an entrenched mode of relating to herself and others with a helplessness that was in fact very important to her. Exploring her investment in her helplessness, developing compassion for her need to make herself helpless, befriending the plight that she faced as a little girl as well as recognizing the resourcefulness she demonstrated in developing this defense were all part of working through this enactment.

Enactments can represent major traumatic experiences (Mia's very early sexual abuse) or subtle modes of relating to self that were organized so early they are both automatic and unconscious (Vita's tendency to relate to herself through punishment and as a helpless victim of circumstances). If we learn to listen for them in the everyday interactions of our patients, we can bring exploration of core issues into the process that may not be otherwise accessible. Ginot (2019) contends that enactments are mutually co-created and therefore intersubjective in nature. "Two subjectivities are triggered by and reacting to each other on a conscious-unconscious continuum" (Ginot, 2019). This understanding alerts us to how we can use the process of monitoring our own contribution as a way to access relational dynamics.

CHAPTER 15

Listening for Organization

L istening for content, feeling, defense, meaning and enactment enables us to access unconscious processes, but there is a type of listening that pervades all of these methods of hearing unconscious wishes, fears and modes of relating. Our minds and brains are *organized* and *organizing* from the moment of conception. Organization manifests itself in fantasy as represented in free associations, feelings, transference, symbolic representation, actions, resistance, and enactments. Transference is vital in helping people understand themselves because it brings within our reach the underlying fantasies, expectations and patterns of relating that organize experience. This organization is unique for everyone and depends on that person's bio/psycho/social history. Organization gives structure to our mental processing. Hanna Segal (1957) was using an organizational framework when she noticed that her patient was equating the coldness of London with the coldness of his mother.

We are listening for organization when we notice recurring patterns of association—for example, that expressions of joy or good feeling are often followed by intimations of impending doom. When we observe that inordinate needs to compete are manifest in the patient's profession, as well as with his wife *and* his children, we are seeing a fundamental organization shaping the patient's experience in many different areas of life. We are seeing organization when we feel so acutely the needs that patients express through the countless little actions of trying to get us to relate to them in a certain way: to tell them what to do, to compete with us, to castrate us, to take care of them, to punish or abuse them. We listen for organization as we listen to a symphony—for the underlying themes, recurring melodies, cross currents of rhythms, emerging and re-emerging voices of different instruments. As mentioned earlier, fantasy carries the organizing dimension of mental activity, one that represents the emotionally based inner narrative of our history. The fundamental way dynamic therapists listen for unconscious process is by listening for underlying organization.

> Edith came to her session after months of dealing with life altering crises. In addition to losing her job, her son (who from infancy had a very low threshold for anxiety) had just started high school and staunchly refused to go. Edith needed to explore treatment options for her son and after almost a year found an anxiety treatment center and then a therapeutic boarding school for him. He is now doing very well. After intensive freelancing and a lengthy job search, she was able to find good employment. The costs associated with her son's treatment were so high, however, that the family needed to sell their apartment and move to a different one in a less expensive part of the city. Finally, she was able to get her daughter off to college where she, too, appears to be doing well.

Edith came to her session remarking that she now knows that life is full of crises and challenges and that she recognizes that a perfect world does not exist. She says that she thinks she has handled the last couple of years very well, but that she also thinks that there is something radically wrong. Instead of feeling good, even joyful about all that she was able to accomplish, Edith felt anxious and depressed, in her words, "like turning inward and hiding inside myself." She knew that she should be feeling better, but just didn't. Close to tears, she said that in fact, she felt awful, "Like hiding under a rock." And she curled up inside herself into an almost fetal position on the couch. The image of hiding herself presented itself repeatedly. It was a repetition of an organization in her mind: hiding inside herself, hiding under a rock and perhaps most evocatively the way she hid her body physically from me, curled up on the couch. I asked myself, "What is all this hiding about? What is she hiding? Who is she hiding from? In what way does she feel that she needs to hide from me? Why does doing well make her feel like hiding under a rock?" I was both curious and felt an impulse to cradle her, as if she were a small, frightened child. I waited for her to resume.

Edith then spoke of how a sense of having to hide her achievements triggered anxiety. She remarked, "I hate to sound like a Freudian textbook (Edith is not a therapist), but I think I'm hiding from my mother's rage at having a special relationship with my father." Edith went on to talk about how when she was a child, her primary connection was with her father. (Her mother clearly preferred her intellectual sister, while her father "played music" with Edith—she played the piano, he the violin). He also appreciated her artistic gifts. Her relationship with her mother, on the other hand, was disconnected, cold and unsatisfying. She remembered overhearing her father asking her mother if she, the mother, loved Edith at all. Her relationship with her mother, internally and externally, was fraught with desperate pleas for love, recognition, and acknowledgment that were largely unrequited.)

But in this session, Edith focused on a different aspect of her relationship with her mother: the way she felt she had to hide her connection with her father from her mother. Her recent triumphs in her career, dealing with her son's problems, launching her daughter in college carried for her the *structure of an Oedipal victory*. These victories triggered fears and fantasies of retribution, ultimately for winning the competition for her father from her mother. This structure was represented in her mind as the idea that adult accomplishment was a triumph over her mother and therefore would bring upon her murderous rage—clearly to her, a danger to be avoided. This idea incited fantasies of her mother's jealousy as well as Edith's powerful wishes to annihilate her. She had a lot to hide from.

As we listen to the content, feeling, defense, meaning, enactments and our own experience, patterns of organization emerge. Developing a sense for the patient's unique organization allows us to understand the emotionally-based structure of experience, no matter what is being talked about. Patients could be discussing their relationships, dreams, experience of self or the therapist, fears or defenses, whatever is coming up in the session. If we listen carefully, we will be able to apprehend the inner structure of that experience. It will echo in a certain way, calling to mind a particular organization, a structure unique to this patient's development. We have all noticed this when we remark to ourselves that this co-worker always seems to feel that she's not getting what she deserves, or that co-worker seems to feel entitled to special treatment no matter what the circumstances.

> A more specific example: A patient, Donna, whose mother "dropped her like a hot potato" at 17 months old when her baby brother was born does not remember this experience. But she is convinced that her boyfriend is going to "drop" her if she says or does the wrong thing. We see in this experience the traumatic memory of being abandoned by someone you love, being helpless to prevent it, and imagining that the reason it happened is that you did something wrong—said or did the "wrong" thing. The emotional triggering was apparent even in talking about her fear, as she moved quickly into the devastating, destabilizing feeling that she would not be able to survive the loss. It would do no good at this point to remind the patient that she survived the loss of her previous boyfriend—a situation from which she also thought she would not recover. Instead, we can help the patient to see that these feelings, intense as they are, are the very feelings she experienced as a tiny little child: the unbearable loss, the helplessness, the ideas she developed that this horrible thing that happened was her fault. These are very real feelings, but they only tangentially belong to a present where the patient's boyfriend truly cares for her, and where she has many more resources than she did when she was two. Helping the patient to gain some distance from the early feelings and impulses that threaten to hijack integrative functioning is an action that

enhances developing observing ego functions. This action simultaneously pulls the patient's attention away from the emotional storm and into more balanced functioning. Getting to this place therapeutically is facilitated by together developing an awareness of the organizational patterns manifest in the patient's relationship to self and others.

We get to see our patient's organizational structure through patients' fantasies—the expectations, demands and ideas they reveal in their modes of relating.

Kevin came back to treatment after twenty years, very disturbed that he was beginning to again have intense anxiety attacks, attacks that he thought he had recovered from. His call to seek therapy was rooted in a panic attack he had had at the hardware store, one that was especially disturbing to him because he had had to reveal his distress to the store manager and to be driven home. We began treatment, and as we discussed the management of his anxiety, what became especially clear was the way Kevin was relating to himself about his resurgence of anxiety. Throughout the course of about three sessions, Kevin remarked about how frustrated and disappointed he was with himself that he was feeling these feelings again. "I thought I was over this!" he would exclaim in disgust, perhaps with some blame directed at his former therapy with me. Repetition is a signpost of organization, and so the repetition of this mode of relating to himself alerted me to the possibility that there was an inner organization that we might need to examine more closely.

First, however, I wanted to make sure that Kevin's impatience wasn't a reflection of lack of knowledge about the nature of anxiety. Although twenty years had passed and I did not remember exactly how we had discussed his anxiety then, I reminded him that it was the nature of anxiety for it to come back, and that he was making unreasonable demands on himself to expect that he should be "cured" of it. As I suspected, this was not a question of lack of knowledge. Kevin understood this. His mode of relating to himself was showing us a powerful fantasy, expressed in the repetition of an enactment that carried meaning for him. His fantasy-driven experience of frustration and disappointment, his expecting that he should have done better was there because it was important to him. Until we work on understanding this importance, his experience will not change.

The next time in the session he brought up his frustration with himself I made the observation that this frustration came up a lot and with palpable intensity. I wondered aloud if feeling this way, disgusted and frustrated with himself, was important to him. Kevin was a little taken aback because he hated feeling this way and wanted nothing more than to feel better. I commented, using the active voice, because Kevin tended to think of himself as a victim, "Yes, you want to feel like you are doing better, but time and again you bring to your mind the idea of not being good enough." This interaction enabled us to explore a piece of Kevin's history that was haunting him: his younger brother was the smart one in the family, brilliant, in fact, and Kevin always felt that compared with his brother he was not good enough. Nobody in his family had ever said this to him, but Kevin levied this charge against himself at every opportunity. A powerful unconscious fantasy developed when as a child he began to see the differences between himself and his brother. His childhood ideas about these differences had organized Kevin's mode of relating to himself and structured his inner world. Seeing and feeling Kevin's mental organization, the way his primary self-engagement was involved with castigating himself, allowed me to understand how to direct my interventions.

Kevin's mental organization became structured by the thousands of moments in which he related to himself while he watched how his brother was related to. His conclusions about what all this meant were necessarily limited by his being a child when they were developed. The psyche's organization is set in place by the ideas, expectations and fantasies of children who operate primarily from an emotionally dominated dimension where the ability to think is necessarily limited. We learn to see organization by looking for the meaning and patterns revealed in how patients relate to us, others and themselves.

PART IV

Changing How Patients Relate to Childhood Trauma and Adversity

"Action without vision is only passing time; vision without action is merely day dreaming, but vision with action can change the world."
— Nelson Mandela and Joel A. Barker

As we approach the end of our journey, we have a greater appreciation for the fact that the largest share of our interaction with patients involves listening, observing, noticing, exploring and reflecting on experience. We listen for the many layers of latent content to better understand how the patient's mind is organized and how their relatedness is structured. Understanding the patient's mental organization provides us with a map that points us to where trauma is buried and where interventions can be most effective. Psychodynamic understanding enables patient and therapist to access patterns of relating that automatically and unconsciously direct experience. Exploring these mental maps, which are shaped by the fears, conflicts and split off parts of self embedded in them, points us directly to those aspects of experience that need therapeutic attention.

The remembering of traumatic experiences has been conserved by evolution because it has predictive and survival value. This can not be changed. We also cannot erase a history of abuse, neglect and problems with attachment. But even though we cannot change the fact of traumatizing adversity in patients' histories, we *can* help them change *how they relate* to these complex developmental traumas, especially to the traces of them that pervade everyday experience. *Working on the tiny manifestations of split-off functioning is key to creating lasting change.* Change lives in the small steps that make up daily life. Noticing the intensity and pervasiveness of the effects of Kevin's mode of relating to himself enabled us to zero in on a powerful and ingrained mode of enacting childhood defenses that had far-reaching consequences. It enabled him to take charge of his life rather than ceding that authority to his feelings of anxiety.

Change is generally not dramatic although at times, "Ah-ha" moments do accompany the insights gained in therapy. The shifts that occur in these moments need to be supported by the less glamorous everyday work of building a new foundation in the integrated centered self. Rewiring the brain requires the support of a strong foundation, one that is constructed, brick by brick, through the laying down of small actions that are strengthened by the mortar of compassionate relating.

Clinically, this is seen in a patient with social anxiety winning a small victory against her impulse to avoid social contact by deciding in favor of meeting up with a friend. Her action is supported by her understanding that the avoidance will only make her more afraid. The action she takes is a concrete instance of restructuring mental organization by building through small steps a change in her neural networks. This kind of mental restructuring is manifest when a patient gives himself time, allowing a space for reflection so that he can see what is going on inside, rather than proceeding along his accustomed route and immediately lashing out when a partner says something hurtful. It is there in therapy sessions when patients risk letting themselves see and feel a thought or feeling they generally ward off. In Kevin's therapy, taking a moment to reflect on how he was invested in relating to himself in the ways he was so used to was central in developing a new relationship to his emotional activation.

Every day offers countless moments in which patients can take the risk of practicing new ways of relating to self and others. These small actions need to be repeated to wire-in the new, more integrated mode of relating. Making a change involves many small steps and small moments. It especially requires being able to appreciate tiny advances. Change can only be accomplished step by step, moment by moment, in connection with the balanced centered self. This integrating connection with self has room for thinking, feeling, memories, anticipations and considered deliberation. These steps towards a more balanced centered self can be celebrated with patients for the victories they are. They are at the heart of patients changing how they relate to the strategies and beliefs they developed as children to deal with what they were not able to assimilate at the time. I will say more about this process in the final chapter of the book.

It is helpful to think of traces of complex developmental trauma as operative on a continuum: sometimes these traces produce a twinge of recognition that something is being activated, a marker so small that the person can easily stay connected with their core centered sense of self. At the higher end of the spectrum, the experience can be more like an alien invasion (an invasion of the body snatchers) in which the patient's usual sense of self is reduced to a discarded shell as intrusive thoughts and feelings take over normal integrated functioning. Keeping this spectrum of activation in mind can help us engage the patient, whenever possible, when activation is at the lower end of the spectrum. It is at the lower end of the spectrum of activation where some of the most productive work will take place. Being on the lower end can allow the patient to examine emotional activation, along with the fears, defenses, strategies and fantasies that propel the arousal, without losing observing ego functions and the capacity for integration. These small changes that mitigate threats to the person's sense of self facilitate integration, one of the goals of psychodynamic treatment.

Three primary considerations will weave through the final chapters of this book. First, working with the intrapsychic dimension of experience; second, the necessity of helping the patient develop observing ego functions; third, facilitating integration.

Relationships are among the most important and richly rewarding aspects of our lives as humans. They transmit our past, organize our present and carry the hopes and dreams we have for the future. They enable a synergistic meeting of minds that gives birth to new visions, thoughts and opportunities. Relationships enrich us. But often, as we survey our relationships, we do not even think about the relationship we have with ourselves. We also may not think about the relationships patients have with themselves. Nothing is more important. No one else can know the secret wishes and fears hidden in the recesses of our minds. We use our relatedness to ourselves to tune us in to the feelings and fantasies that are stimulated in our relationship with patients. Being able to notice the intrapsychic dimension of our patients' relatedness to themselves helps us to see their internal mental organization. Relatedness to self, the connectedness and disconnectedness patients and therapists develop with their inner worlds help us to understand relatedness to others. The interconnectedness of mental processing, its responsivity to inner and outer stimulation, insures that memories of the past will organize our relationships in the present, with others as well as with ourselves.

Throughout the final three chapters, I will be examining in more detail how patients relate to themselves, the *intrapsychic* dimension of relating. Mental organization is fueled by a rich tapestry of the interaction between internal and external relatedness. A history of abuse, for example will sensitize certain patients to the abusive potential in others, and may also activate a tendency to abuse the self.

Relating through abuse (being abused or abusing others) can also become the primary way the patient feels connected. For example, the patient may actively stimulate abusive behavior in order to obtain an emotional reconnection (with themselves and others) that other modes of relating do not provide. Because affect is an intrinsic aspect of relatedness, we look for it in intrapsychic and interpersonal interactions. Affects are always present and directing us to what is most meaningful.

Our minds are formed in relation to others during the earliest years of our lives. Our early interactions with self and others create patterns between intrapsychic and interpersonal experience that influence each other. These intrapsychic and interpersonal dimensions tend to blend into each other, especially in times of stress or emotional triggering. Intrapsychic, fantasy-driven experiences of others—how we perceive them, what they symbolize for us, what defenses are stimulated by them—are significant components of how we perceive and relate to others. When we are operating from an open and flexible sense of self, we are able to "see" and let in more of the "otherness" of the other person (Ginot 2015). When, for whatever reasons, we are less open and flexible, when we are on the alert or expecting danger, protective functions are activated, and defensive fantasies may dominate the interpersonal interaction.

We are relating to ourselves all the time. We may check in with ourselves to see if we are hungry, if we would like a cold beer or a hot date, or if we *really* need to get that paper read for class. Much of how we relate to ourselves does not fall under the category of unconscious enactment. But a good deal of it does. Ideas, beliefs, feelings and fantasies that are more rigidly held, those that are more entwined with defense and less integrated into one's centered sense of self, often carry unconscious intrapsychic enactments, organized modes of relating to different aspects of self that embody split-off fantasies, meaning and feeling. Listening for how patients are relating *to themselves* gives us opportunities to identify and clarify early unconscious, unmetabolized patterns of relating that have a significant impact on the patient's life.

I worked with Jenny for a number of years. The treatment was focused primarily on a childhood that was emotionally very painful. Her father, a teacher, demonstrated his caring primarily through excessive demands for her to do more and more schoolwork and to get the best grades. He barely spoke with her outside his involvement with her school-work, which was never good enough. Her mother, a beauti-ful, anxious, rather narcissistic woman, was extraordinarily unresponsive to Jenny's physical or emotional sensitivities, scrubbing her with a hard brush until she was screaming in agony, and ignoring Jenny's wails that the bathwater was scalding hot. Typically, they would quarrel every morning and Jenny would walk to school in tears, wearing dirty clothes and shoes. Only when she was ill did Jenny's mother give her the care and solicitude that she so deeply longed for every day. Perhaps the most painful experience for Jenny was when mother and father would retire to their bedroom after dinner and lock their door, leaving Jenny to do homework and housework, and to care for herself for the rest of the night. Her situation was made especially difficult by her overhearing the gaiety and laughter com-ing from her parent's bedroom. Jenny felt locked out of what she deeply yearned for: emotional connection with her parents. To make matters even more difficult, when Jenny would ask for something from her parents—a dress, a toy, time to play with a parent or friends, a book or even a birthday present (she never had a party)—she was told they couldn't afford anything or that she was asking for too much.

Jenny was quite depressed when she started treatment. But she was committed to the process. We worked on under-standing her history and developing a narrative connect-ing her early experience to her current feelings. Over the years she developed a good life. She married a man who loved her and treated her well, developed good relationships with others, became a professional who was valued in her field, and after a time had a child of her own, a son. It appeared that despite the adversity of her early life, things were going well.

I was therefore not prepared when during a regular session Jenny confided in me that she had been deeply dissociated, that she had felt profoundly cut off from herself for weeks. She felt disconnected from herself and her family, and she was using television and her smartphone to disengage from her feelings. A sense of guilt and shame about her history dominated her experience. When we examined what those feelings were, we saw that Jenny blamed herself for her troubled early life. A deep, quiet depression emerged. She did not want to live. She acknowledged that she had her husband and her baby, but she couldn't stop her dissociating or thinking about the neglect and abuse of her childhood. Her childhood and her feelings of depression, neglect and self-blame shamed her so much that she didn't see how she could go on. Jenny was serious. I had never seen her so despondent.

In this session, our exploration led her to confide much more than she previously had about the depth of her childhood despair. Although Jenny had told me how unhappy she had been as a child, she had not been able to convey how emotionally overwhelming it was and to fully communicate the depth of her suffering. Jenny confided now that she had, in fact, been suicidal during her childhood. She had not wanted to live. Perhaps the only thing that connected her to life at the time was the fact that her high ability was recognized at school. There she felt valued. But remembering her childhood despair now brought it all back with a vengeance and a conviction that I had known only more distantly before. Now I could see and feel and taste her despair at every moment. I had the fantasy that although she had told me about her childhood experience, now she felt safe enough with me to actually let me share it with her viscerally. There was no mistaking the deep intensity of the feelings that now dominated her experience. I could see that she was reliving her childhood trauma in the present. Mostly I just listened to the outpouring of her sadness. I made the observation that she was now showing me the full intensity of the feelings she had as a child. I was trying to help give her more distance from the yawning chasm of depression that threatened to swallow her up. Jenny acknowledged that she needed me to see and feel the full intensity of her despair, but it was clear to both of us that we would have to end the session without resolution of this painful experience. I told her that she could let me know if she needed an extra session; I wanted her to know that she had my support, that I was there for her. She thanked me but did not call. I was concerned.

At our next session, Jenny was still in a dark place. In tears, she said, "I know my parents loved me, but I don't know the feeling of being loved. It's like a fruit I have never tasted." She next thought about her husband, remarking that he can love. "It's so simple for him." Jenny continued, "Connecting with others is easy for him. The hardest step is to love yourself." Jenny zeroed in on a primary component that was driving her despair: a mode of relating to herself that was both destructively critical and hopeless, one that mirrored and enacted intrapsychically her early relationship with her parents.

Focusing on how patients *relate to themselves* has therapeutic value. As a gateway to the patient's unconscious relational system, intrapsychic functioning provides us with opportunities to see, examine and bring problematic modes of relating directly the room. My patient Jenny, who as a child lived with an extreme level of parental unpredictability and emotional neglect, found it very difficult to extend periods of feeling good beyond a couple of weeks, the maximum length of time during which her father related to her with care and kindness. She related to herself on the same schedule and in the same mode in which she was related to as a child.

Another productive focus involves simply noticing the tone of voice with which a patient speaks about himself. Our observation can provide a moment for reflection on a pattern of relating to self that is so habitual it doesn't even register. Like an unpleasant odor they've adapted to and stopped noticing, patients typically are not conscious of many negative modes of relating to self, however destructive they may be. On a pragmatic level, because patients are relating to themselves at every moment, developing a deeper understanding of their modes of relating provides them with countless opportunities for working them through in the course of every day. Many intrapsychic enactments, fantasies and patterns of relating are the products of trauma (including neglect, abuse and conflictual attachment). Opportunities are always at hand to practice identifying, tolerating and accepting these patterns in order to work on befriending new ways of relating, and so intensifying the healing process.

The process of free association gives us many openings to see how patients relate to themselves. Do they inhibit themselves, bottling themselves up so that not even a word can escape? Do they flood the therapist with facts and feelings that seem to have no end? Do they give themselves permission to reflect on their experience? Do they relate to themselves with caring consideration and kindness or with critical judgmentalness? Do they characteristically dredge up bad feelings after revealing good ones? Listening for the emotional meaning of how patients connect *with* themselves or disconnect *from* themselves shows us a vital facet of their psychic organization. Affect connects us to core internal and external dimensions of experience that allow us to address primary organization. Intrapsychic and interpersonal dimensions of experience are central processes involved in the experiencing and projection of affect, different facets of how core emotional subjectivity (fantasy, wishes, fears, etc.) organizes experience. One dimension becomes the foreground of therapeutic work only to recede into the background at other times. Keeping in mind the interconnection between intrapsychic and interpersonal modes of relating, and the way that emotional experience infuses our inner and outer lives enables us to more clearly see the patient's mental organization as well as the way we (intersubjectively) stimulate each other.

Reflection is an intrapsychic process, a looking inside at how one is experiencing oneself, the therapist or others. In addition to reflection, we have spoken about the way in which *actions* can be a vehicle through which intrapsychic organization can be identified. When I speak of an *intrapsychic enactment*, I am referring to an automated, emotionally driven, less conscious mode of relating to the self, such as Jenny's critical and hopeless way of connecting with herself.

Interpersonal enactments involve unconscious actions that are developed or taken *within the therapeutic relationship or with others*. Interactions with intimate others (husbands and wives, parents and children, siblings, and so on) are particularly vulnerable to the emergence of enactments and a fusion of intrapsychic and interpersonal modes of relating. In the treatment situation, the therapist becomes an intimate other, a target for the longings, fears and fantasies that organize experience. Interpersonal enactments carry representations of specific intrapsychic processing, how the patient relates to self. A patient with a tendency to punish herself by berating herself for not being perfect, for example, may stimulate and enact fantasies of punishment in the therapeutic interaction. In these situations, the therapist may in fact be stimulated to play the role of the punisher. Or conversely, the therapist may be emotionally activated to take the role of the punished. Being able to pick up on these inner dynamics as they are represented in the interpersonal world can help us to better see how they are organized and played out in the patient's intrapsychic world. And examining the patient's intrapsychic world can also help us to better understand the patient's interpersonal modes relating. The interconnectedness of mental functions ensures that we can look for inner organization in many aspects of the patient's relatedness.

In ordinary functioning, the emotional meaning of internal and external situations moves us toward our goals. Situations that activate emotional triggering, on the other hand, often generate a takeover by early, emotionally dominated functioning. Triggered emotionality takes the helm, instead of emotion connecting us to meaningful activity. For example, during times of stress a patient might respond to his partner with an eruption of hostility: *"Why are you always pushing me to do exactly what you want the moment you want it?"* When a sense of urgency and conviction displaces the ability to wait, or to communicate more effectively, a transference enactment is emerging. We are pulled out of our centered state into a timeless vortex that threatens to swallow us up.

Working with small traces of emotional activation, what we might call micro-trauma triggering, enables patients to capture split-off aspects of self while they are still connected to the centered, integrated aspect of themselves. These milder traces of early experience enable us to identify defenses, enactments and symbolic processes *before* splitting processes activate emotional hijacking. Developing a patient's facility to see and work with these small aspects of mental processing gives them an invaluable tool in changing how they relate to emotional triggering. It provides them with countless opportunities to be active and in charge when relating to these inner aspects of functioning. Acting when ego functioning is more integrated enables split-off aspects of self to engage observing ego functions. Patients thereby connect to central aspects of self even as they allow themselves to see and hear what other parts of themselves are trying to communicate.

Supporting the emergence of an observing ego, an aspect of self that can stand with but not be overwhelmed by trauma-infused feelings, is critical to trauma recovery. Van der Kolk (2014) emphasizes that trauma recovery involves helping patients to change their relationship with trauma activation in order "to learn to live with the memories of the past without being overwhelmed by them in the present" (p. 279). Helping patients observe and notice (from a calm, centered state) their emergent experience *as an object of interest* is an essential aspect of change. A stronger observing ego transforms the patient's relationship to triggering incidents. When this is achieved (a facility that is developed slowly in the presence of a safe and trusting relationship with the therapist), the patient no longer experiences the trauma reminder as something dreadful that is about to happen in the present. The overwhelming terror of retraumatization is replaced by a realization that a certain kind of feeling is being activated. Noticing experience as an object of curiosity enables patients to distance themselves from the memories, defenses and fantasies associated with traumatizing childhood experiences. This, in and of itself, leaves patients feeling safer. It effects a change in their relationship to their emotional trigger. This optimal distance facilitates integration.

Many approaches have evolved to help people change how they relate to the automatic emotional arousal connected with complex developmental trauma. Although some of these approaches are not psychodynamic, most of them share common components with psychodynamic principles and all of them *involve creating an environment in which cultivating integration and furthering observing-ego capacities are central facets.* Meditation, yoga, and sensory focused healing combine relaxation with focused awareness. Internal Family Systems therapy, developed by Richard Schwartz, is another approach to trauma treatment that *integrates intrapsychic and interpersonal experience* (Goulding and Schwartz, 1995). A calm enough state in which one is able to reflect on inner experience is a common denominator. Within a psychodynamic perspective, one example among many, is Fred Busch's work (2016) with patients' defensive functioning. Characteristic of his approach is that he asks patients to stop and notice what was going on in their minds as they hesitate or interrupt their associative flow. Busch is asking patients to step back during a moment of mild emotional activation and to observe their own processes, to shift their perspective. Focusing on identifying and working with small manifestations of early problematic modes of relating involves structuring the therapeutic process in a way that enhances the observing-ego functions of therapist and patient alike. As we work in this way, both collaborators in the process are more able to notice split-off impulses, actions, demands, fears, and fantasies. This noticing allows the patient to actively connect the dots, enhancing personal agency. Attending to incidents on the lower levels of emotional activation and the structural similarities between present functioning and traumatizing childhood experiences gives us access to mental organization and processing that may otherwise be sealed off from our engagement.

CHAPTER 16

Identifying Emotional Triggers

On the surface, identifying emotional triggers seems a straightforward task. A patient reacts to a situation with an emotional response that does not "fit" the situation in appropriateness, intensity, tenacity, capriciousness, or ambivalence (Greenson, 1968). (A woman's performance on the job is questioned and she breaks down in tears of self-hatred. A man becomes irrationally jealous when his wife is courteous to a colleague. A designer is paralyzed when her boss suggests an alternative concept for her project.) But emotional activation can be much more subtle, and dissociative processes can obscure significant defenses. Emotional triggers can involve silently cutting off, blaming self or others, subtly changing the topic or a limitless host of other possibilities. Emotional triggers may be consciously apprehended by the patient as alien or so intertwined with the patient's sense of self that the triggers feel like a vital aspect of themselves. Not all emotional triggers come with emotional storms. With some patients it is more a question of a shift in the direction of the wind.

Some therapists feel that taking a patient's history can alert one to specific issues that will come up in the treatment. Not uncommonly, if the therapist works for a clinic, hospital or institute, having the patient fill out a form, checklist or description of their history is required. There is considerable debate about when and how to take a patient's history. It can be done at the beginning of a treatment, which allows the therapist to have a better sense of underlying issues and possible areas of emotional activation. If we have patience, however, and the freedom to keep the importance of uncovering the history in mind, it can be more productive to use our curiosity to gather the history as it emerges rather than to "take" a history all at once. There are important reasons for this.

First, especially with patients who have experienced complex developmental trauma, we want to give the patient as much control over the process as he or she needs. We do not want to interrupt the patient's timing or sequencing in order to satisfy our need to know as quickly as possible. When we are in a data-driven frame of mind, looking only for the conscious, external answers a patient can supply at the beginning of a treatment, we lose the possibility of seeing and helping the patient to explore the fantasies, feelings and associations that may emerge in the telling. This impacts the degree to which we can see emotional arousal in vivo and begin together to make connections between past experience and present functioning.

Second, we need to acknowledge that there is much inside the patient that we are not yet aware of. The action of pursuing our agenda usurps the patient's process. We risk losing the moment when many internal factors come together and are ready to be expressed to the therapist. Respecting a patient's readiness, or lack of readiness, is a way to communicate that we value our patient's process and are willing to wait for the time that is right for them. Respect for the patient's sequencing is a significant factor with patients who have traumatic developmental histories, because providing them with opportunities to be in charge is part of the recovery process.

Third, psychodynamic work involves staying as close to the patient's process as we can, because this allows us to see more clearly the currents of organization, feeling and meaning that pervade experience. Direct questions and answers that keep the patient responding to us rather than attending to their inner reflections do not help us to see or enter the patient's world. An approach that recognizes the importance of the patient's history in the organization of wishes, fears, and fantasies, will find ample opportunities to be curious about the details of the patient's experience in ways that build reflection about that history into the process.

Careful listening for associations that are freighted with latent meaning, staying connected to the sense of how the patient experiences the therapist, watching for changes in bodily expression, listening for the unsaid, working with the patient's resistance and dreams all point us to the patient's emotional triggers. This is slow and painstaking work for many reasons, not the least of which is that it takes time to understand a person's mental organization. Moreover, our primary goal is to stay connected with the patient. If we get too far ahead, feelings of disconnection or abandonment can be stimulated. Focusing only on the content can lead us to miss emotional cues and take us down dead ends. Accurately perceiving the experience of another person takes time and careful listening. When beginning a treatment, we know little about the patient. Openness to the full experience of the patient by attending to the patient's words, tone, non-verbal cues and actions allows for the most productive type of listening for emotional activation.

The following example helps us to see how more obvious traumatic losses can hide earlier complex developmental issues that profoundly influence the process of emotional triggering.

Vita was a high-powered attorney working for a major corporation until it went under. Being laid off work was extremely challenging for Vita since much of her identity was anchored in being the breadwinner, her knowing that she was the one who could provide her family with financial stability. The intensity of her reaction to her job loss (her anguish and dread over it drove her into treatment) suggested to me that she was being emotionally triggered.

Vita's mother had died of cancer when Vita was 10 years old. She was the oldest of four children closely spaced in age. The father had a hard time dealing with his wife's death, and after she died, was not able to be emotionally present for the children. The family struggled for many years. During this time, Vita envied her friends who came from stable, secure homes and vowed to herself that she would study hard and become an attorney like one of her friend's parents, so that she would be able to have security in the future. She drove herself mercilessly until she was accepted into University and landed a position at a top law firm. Her anxiety after losing her job was tied to the powerless feelings she had as a child after her mother's death. Her more prominent defenses included a relentless badgering of herself to do more—a mode of relating to herself that was primitive and brutal in its intensity. Also in evidence were the denial, dissociation and splitting defenses that she used to ward off the trauma of feeling so helplessly alone after her mother's death. We worked productively on connecting with feelings she had buried for many years and becoming more aware of her emotional triggers. During this time, she developed a software program, a product with high value in today's financial marketplace. She was able to rank among the finalists in efforts to sell it to major international corporations, but despite significant interest, she was not able to close a deal.

Vita decided to look for a job. But she couldn't fully commit to putting herself out there. Time and again she would report that she didn't make a call she needed to make, that she procrastinated doing the things she wanted to do, and that she just couldn't bear the whole process. At first, I was puzzled. I could see how much she had grown in the last couple of years emotionally and professionally. She had developed expertise in an area that was hungry for people with her knowledge and skills. But as she talked about the misery she experienced looking for a job, I noticed how negatively and hopelessly she compared herself with other job contenders. Whether she was up against real companies who were competing for the same work or imagined individual rivals, her fantasy of herself was consistently one of being small and inadequate, unable to make the grade, and hopelessly outclassed.

I began to notice more how seeing herself negatively in comparison with others was an automatic and unconscious habit for Vita. I remembered in the back of my mind how Vita had asked seemingly offhand questions about how others manage these types of problems. Images of sibling rivalry began to emerge. I began to ask more about her experience with her siblings: how much time elapsed between her birth and the birth of each of her three siblings? What were her earliest memories of her siblings? How was the connection with her mother during this time? With quiet tears Vita told me that there wasn't much time at all. They were all about a year and a half apart in age. Gradually, as we focused more on this earliest period in her life, we discovered that the death of her mother was her *second* trauma. The first was the loss of her mother that she experienced over and over again with the birth of each sibling beginning when she was just 18 months old. The obvious and more consciously held memory of the trauma she endured with the death of her mother was a *crystallization*, a screen memory of a much earlier one: the complex developmental trauma she faced as a very small child who was desperately trying to reconnect with the mother she once had, the mother she had lost when her siblings started their relentless march into her life. Because she was so young, her explanations of why she felt so isolated, alone and inadequate focused on her childhood idea that she was not good enough. With a child's logic she imagined that if she could only make herself perfect, if she could just "peddle faster" she might fare better. Even though her siblings were all younger, they seemed to her (like the fantasized rivals for jobs in the present) to have the power, connections and confidence that she sorely lacked.

We have been working on this issue and it is becoming clearer to Vita why she responds as she does to situations that evoke memories of the hopeless feelings connected with these overwhelming and impossible rivalries she suffered as a little girl. Vita's helpless hopelessness as a child generated ideas that the losses she endured were her fault and that, if she worked harder at being better, she might be able to recover what she had lost.

Despite the expertise she has developed in her field, the evidence that she is valued in the marketplace, and her high intelligence, there are still times when her early feelings and fantasies trigger her profoundly. At these times, she is so convinced of the "rightness" of her feeling that she becomes almost paralyzed by the emotional conviction that she is far outclassed by and inferior to others. The intensity, disproportionateness, and hopelessness of her reaction, generated by childhood experience and her fantasy of needing to be perfect in order to compete, is consistent with an understanding that she is suffering from complex developmental trauma. This early trauma is repeatedly re-experienced, as situations that remind her of this difficult time in her early life activate feelings and memories that overwhelm her. When triggered, Vita is operating with the emotional conviction supplied by her now dominant right brain, and she uses the "strategies" she developed as a child to deal with her emotional arousal. At the same time, her left brain, (her keen logical, systemic and analytic ability) has been rendered a lifeless shell and is nowhere to be found.

As we work with patients who have experienced complex developmental trauma, we learn to differentiate the early signs of moving into emotional arousal. Sometimes tone of voice can be a marker; often there are specific words (typically judgmental ones, such as "You jerk," or "you idiot," etc.) or certain phrases or ways of talking to oneself. At times, the signal of moving toward an activated response is carried by the patient starting to compare himself with others. One of the goals of helping patients to change how they relate to emotional triggers is to work with them to identify the precursors of emotional activation *before* they move into a full-blown emotional hijacking by right-brain dominated emotional processing. The signals of moving toward emotional hijacking are going to be different for every patient. It takes conscientious and collaborative work to identify the signals that can be used to alert patients that they are about to get sucked into the vortex. As understanding and recognition of these signals are developed, patient and therapist together can check with each other when they hear an outcropping of arousal related experience.

My patient, Kevin, was wedded to the idea that he did not perform as well as most people. As we explored the reasons for this conviction about himself, he began to see how his childhood explanations for the problems in his family of origin were "useful" to him, even though his sense of self suffered terribly in the process. We spent a good deal of time exploring the minute processes that engaged him as he sped down the slippery path to full-on emotional activation. This exploration had to be done before or after, not during the arousal. Sometimes it could be approached before a triggering as I asked him to imagine how he was relating to himself and to share that with me. From these examinations of the process, we were able to generate a list of words, a tone (contempt), mode of relating (self-blame) and content (comparing himself unfavorably with others) that we could use in future battles with his automatic, unconscious early enactments.

We learn to hear emotional triggering especially in the tone of the patient's communication. Use of words, phrases, tone or actions that convey a sense of urgency or desperation are often indicators that very early experience is getting activated. When a patient sucks in her breath in fear or uses words or phrases that convey a sense of urgency, we do well to ask ourselves and our patients what is going on. While there are some situations in an adult's life that involve life or death circumstances, generally speaking these feelings belong to a much earlier time. This type of thinking is indicative of an epoch in which black and white thinking predominated and the patient actually was much more helpless when facing a threatening situation. The experience of urgency, helplessness, hopelessness and desperation generally carry an infusion of early trauma or profound adversity. It is primarily children who feel desperate and helpless because their autonomy in the world is limited — for many years they must depend on adults to take care of their needs. Attending to the quality of the patient's communication and using our curiosity to actively examine and explore the patient's associations to this quality can lead us directly to the heart of significant emotional issues.

A useful tool in identifying emotional activation and the triggering that can accompany it is to be curious about *when* the current feeling in question emerged. How long has the patient been feeling anxious, enraged, depressed, overwhelmed, suicidal, etc.? The timing of when a feeling emerges and the context of what it is connected to often point to a symbolic resonance that is useful to explore therapeutically. We saw this when we were talking about the transference/countertransference activity of my patient Edith who had trouble comforting herself unless she was overwhelmed. Asking her if she could identify when her anxiety emerged in the present allowed her to point to the time when her last child went off to college, a time when her defense of being "busy, busy, busy" was less effective, making it more possible to turn her gaze inward. Before therapy, patients often do not take the time to reflect on what was going on when they become emotionally activated. We can do this work with them, helping them to learn how to connect the dots and understand the emotional connections.

Not uncommonly, we have trouble identifying emotional triggers because we do not have the relevant information. Patients often tell us about their experience with less than the intimate detail we need to see what is going on. We cannot do our work based on abstractions or foregone conclusions. We need to see and hear all the details in order to catch the underlying patterns that may be activating emotional arousal. Asking the patient for a detailed description of what was going on right before they became emotionally activated can begin the process of enabling both parties to see more clearly what was stimulating the emotional arousal.

The intimate interpersonal dimensions of the therapeutic situation inevitably arouse intrapsychic feelings, defenses and fantasies, in both patient and therapist. As therapists, we use our countertransferential awareness to awaken us to the processes that are emerging. We learn to pay attention even to passing thoughts and peripheral fantasies in addition to more developed mental processes. We need to remember that enactments in the therapeutic situation *may or may not* involve the therapist directly. *Patients enact their relatedness to others in how they relate to themselves.* Enactments, like transference, resistance and defense, are all around us; they are representations of how patients organize and process the world.

With patients who have experienced abuse, neglect and disordered attachment, we need to be cognizant of the risk of stimulating these early experiences. Trauma survivors react to the organizational structure of their early relatedness as it is represented in everyday experience. Experiences in the present, including the interaction with the therapist, that are associated with this organization can take on the meaning of the original traumatic experiences. When the original trauma is *powerfully* represented by a pattern of acting or experiencing in the present, it can be interpreted as a re-traumatization. It is also helpful to think of this process on a continuum, with degrees of activation from mild to severe. If there are many points of connection to the original trauma and the activation is intense, the patient is more likely to experience a reliving of the early traumatic experience. Careful listening is listening that stays with the patient. This advice holds especially when the patient needs time to develop a readiness to bear the raw and unintegrated feelings that may surface with emotional exploration.

Identifying the activation of early childhood modes of relating when they are woven into the fabric of the patient's sense of self can be especially challenging. When manifestations of early mental organization fit seamlessly into the patient's experience, they can be hard to identify as emotional triggers. We illustrated the enactment of early modes of organization in our chapter on listening for enactment, when we looked at how, as an adolescent, Susan developed the idea that freedom and relief from the experience of being controlled by her father could be found in binge eating. This childhood strategy empowered her and simultaneously punished her for connecting with herself. It also asserted a loud "Fuck you!" to anyone (including herself or the therapist) who dared to try to control her.

Susan's therapy involved helping her learn how to develop more compassion for the little girl she had been who was trying to balance so many conflicting forces amid her desire to take care of herself. Gradually, she was able to develop more ability to reflect on her experience and to self-regulate, especially when old feelings, fears and beliefs started to surface. In countless encounters, Susan courageously confronted impulses that were at once daunting and commanding, learning bit by bit to befriend the experience her body was holding. Working with not judging herself was necessary. Recognizing when she was punishing herself, and what she got out of punishing herself, was essential. Struggling to ensure safety amid the countless ways she launched herself over the cliff into triggered impulses to punish herself was a core component of the treatment, a treatment in which binge eating was only a part of a larger drama. I realized that we had reached a tipping point when Susan had the following dream:

> I was driving a car going over a bridge above a huge chasm.
> I went through the guard rails and was falling thousands
> of feet in the air to the ground below and would crash at
> the bottom. I thought, well, this is it. I guess this is my time.
> I embraced my death. And as soon as I did, the car turned
> into a plane and I flew off and survived.

We see in Susan's dream that there was a part of herself that was ready to drive herself through the guardrails of her life over a cliff, deep into the abyss. This is clearly a problem, attested to by the visceral image of crashing at the bottom of the chasm. But we also see a part of her that was willing to take control of her life. Embracing her death in her dream was her way of accepting herself, and this enabled her to fly. Her acceptance of herself transformed the inevitability of death into the empowering embrace of her own control in adversity. It took years of undergoing harrowing fears and realities for Susan to have a dream that speaks so clearly to her ability to embody *and* accept her punishing, destructive impulse and in so doing, to transform it.

In this example, the work of our compassionate listening to the patient's intrapsychic experience enabled her to reflect more on how she was relating to herself and ultimately to champion her wish to pilot her own life. Identifying her emotional triggers enabled her to regain a balance between the impulsive side of her that pushed her to overeat and the part of herself that wanted to relate to the whole of herself, which involved eating in a more conscious, balanced and healthy way. These real actions of eating in a more caring and healthy way embodied a changing intrapsychic balance that was now driving her experience.

Sometimes emotional triggering needs to be identified through the gradual demonstration of a pattern that has meaning to the patient. For this demonstration to be most effective, the pattern needs to be identified and examined in the therapeutic relationship and connected to how it appears in the patient's relationships with self or others outside of therapy.

Jeannine became aware as she was growing up that her mother identified her with her uncle, the mother's brother, toward whom the mother felt intense rivalry and hatred. As a little girl, Jeannine felt devalued and discarded as, day after day, she endured her mother's unfavorable comparisons. "You're just like your Uncle Charlie," the mother would tell Jeannine with contempt. Jeannine's associations to these experiences included other ways in which she felt with both her mother and father that she was not being heard, remembered or valued for who she was. Her rage and woundedness is easily triggered in the present when she feels snubbed or uncared about by her husband, her colleagues, and, of course, in her transference activity with me. Depending on the intensity of the specter of being devalued, emotional activation can vary considerably. Typically, this patient can hold on to the connection to the therapist when in her presence. After the session, however, fantasies of being abandoned and uncared about usually come to the fore and her rage-filled wounds generate a present day version of her childhood solution—some kind of walking away, often represented by the thought, "I've had enough!" This patient has left several jobs, divorced two husbands, disconnected from several long-term friendships, and discontinued her treatment with me several times.

It was a step toward integration when, in a recent session, after she recognized that I empathized with the pattern of hopelessness and disconnection she gets caught in (with her mother, her husband and her work) that the patient was able to tell me in the session that she had an impulse to end the treatment right there and then. When I asked her to tell me about this, she was initially silent. Then, hesitating, she told me that she felt that I was getting too close, that my understanding about her hopelessness was more than she could bear. "I can't stand feeling that you care about me! . . . I guess if I end things first, then I don't have to worry about being discarded," she admitted. Jeannine was stuck in an enactment of an early defense—being close is too dangerous to bear. It felt safer for Jeannine to cut off the other person and her own desire for closeness because this meant to her that she was not the one who was cut off by the world. In this action, repeated many times in her life, Jeannine identified with the mother's disparagement of the other (the mother's brother and Jeannine) and made herself feel safe by cutting off first, being the one who actively controlled the cutting off. Exploration of this idea, at a stage when her ego was not incapacitated by re-traumatization, led to deepening her understanding of the centrality of this issue and her own role in her complex interactions with others.

The work of identifying emotional triggers is necessarily slow and complex. It requires countless repetitions to help the patient change the potentiation of neural networks that are automatically activated. Only after we understand that a trauma is being triggered can we begin the work of changing how the trauma is related to in the present.

CHAPTER 17

Developing a Narrative

Collaboratively developing a narrative that links past with present, illuminating the many ways patients learned how to protect themselves from pain, is an essential part of recovering from childhood adversity and trauma. This narrative must make sense to the patient. It pulls the pieces of the puzzle together, helping them to understand why they developed particular modes of relating to self and others, why certain experiences generate such intense feelings. Part of this understanding must include the defensive processes that were established very early, as these patterns of relating become structured into the developing mind. We access these processes in therapy through our focused listening to the patient's dreams, feelings, fantasies, enactments and transference activity. We remember, as we work with developing narratives, that defensive processes are generated well before the child is conscious of self or capable of emotional regulation. They have a childlike quality, often involving splitting or dichotomous thinking. Because these strategies were developed to deal with inescapable and emotionally overwhelming situations, they have become vital to the patient's sense of wellbeing. Understanding the *automaticity* of these defenses and the patient's *attachments* to them helps patients make sense of why changing is so difficult. Compassionate understanding of the challenges they faced as tiny, little children mitigates the self-blame that is so easily triggered as patients work to change how they relate.

As we develop the narrative, we must keep in mind that the therapeutic process of changing entrenched defenses in the present can have a similar organizational structure to the issues with which the patient struggled in the past. For example, the complexities and difficulties involved as Donna worked on changing her conviction that her boyfriend would leave her (just as her mother did when her baby brother came along) can stimulate the re-emergence of the helpless/hopeless feelings she had as a toddler. The emergence of these enactments in the therapeutic process are useful, for they show us in action what the patient cannot remember in images or conscious recollections. Developing a narrative that connects past and present experience enables patients to make sense of and get distance from the unconscious fantasies that connect these experiences. Without the narrative understanding, patients often slip into mistaking memories of early feelings of hopelessness, dread, and urgency for what is going on in the present. Donna, for example, was hijacked at times by the emotional conviction that her boyfriend was truly going to leave her.

On the level of the therapeutic interaction, it is quite common for overwhelming early experiences of helplessness and hopelessness to be activated by the inevitable recalcitrance encountered when patient and therapist work on changing a childhood strategy. The similarity between the helplessness experienced in the early situation and the difficulty experienced in the present when patients are working on changing an unconscious automated defense share an internal structure— one of struggling to attain an outcome that is very difficult to achieve. The difference is that unlike the early situation when the child was indeed often helpless, changing one's response to an old defense is difficult, but it can be done. It requires perseverance, time, and internal struggle, but changing the way we relate to emotional activation is possible. As we work on this demanding task with our patients, we need to be aware that the task itself can be triggering. The difficulty of the therapeutic task can stimulate feelings of shame, guilt, and other fantasies of not being able to accomplish as much as is desired as quickly as it is wanted. Understanding the way that the therapy itself may be triggering early traumatic experience will help us to further develop the narrative. We do this by exploring and examining how the patient is relating to self around the emerging therapeutic challenges.

Helping patients to identify, understand and have compassion for what they needed to do in order to protect themselves is an essential part of working with all patients. How patients relate to the parts of themselves that generated these strategies is especially important. Developing compassion and even admiration for what the little child was able to do to protect herself and to get her needs met is a vital part of the healing process. Children use the only resources they have available: their own bodies and how they relate to self and others. Some kids may learn that keeping silent and smiling will help them to get the love they need; others may find that taking inner control by blaming themselves gives them the relief of turning a situation from one in which they are passive or helpless into one in which they are active or in control; still others may find that misbehaving gets them the emotional connection they hunger for and cannot find in any other way. The possibilities are endless.

Situations that have some similarity to the original trauma will inevitably stimulate the original traumatic situation. This propensity to be triggered, for similarities to activate emotionally based fears, memories and fantasies is a part of the mental framework we develop through our early interactions in the world. Therapy, especially with those who experienced complex developmental trauma or adverse childhood experience, is a process that involves re-wiring the brain, *changing our relationship to what gets emotionally triggered*. Although we cannot change the fact of having experienced trauma (and this reality has far reaching consequences), we can change the *meaning* connected to the feelings that are stimulated by similar situations. We can change our relationship to it.

Treatment of phobias uses this approach all the time. Patients are taught to understand their bodily experience (sweating, pounding heart, anxiety, lightheadedness) as physical reactions to the feared stimulus. They learn that with practice, relaxation and staying centered, these reactions will eventually relent. Instead of feeling that they are going to pass out if they get on a plane, they learn to reinterpret their experience as their body getting activated by a fear reaction. They learn to endure the bodily felt discomfort. Trauma involves the activation of our fear system as well, though the meanings that get evoked with trauma are much more complex and often much more terrifying than simple phobias. In addition, many of the meanings and some fears are not conscious. Changing our relationship to the feelings that are triggered by trauma reminders therefore involves learning to understand and tolerate the unbearable. It includes integrating many aspects of self, including wishes, fears, fantasies, defenses and ideas. Patience in both collaborators is necessary here as these processes take time. Integration is facilitated by developing a narrative understanding with patients of what happened and how they structured relating to themselves and others to deal with the emotional facts of their early lives.

Hope came to her session with the statement: "I had dreams." She went on to tell me: I am at a gathering or conference—a scene not uncommon in my dreams. In this dream I am talking to a girlfriend about going to a makeup counter to get them to tell me what works for me. But I realize that I already have this knowledge. I know what works for me. It was more a matter of bonding with my girlfriend.

Then I am in a class, a French class and my father is visiting, sitting in the back of the class. French was my best subject, but I have not been to the class for a long time. The teacher said that she was missing my homework for a couple of weeks. I had a righteous feeling—I knew all of this and besides I knew I had turned in some of the homework. But the teacher was very stern with me. She was very depressed and very stern, letting me know how bad I was. That was the end of the dream.

She continues: My immediate association is to a women's group I went to a few weeks ago at which I felt absolutely mortified (this was her first appointment after a two-week holiday break). Hope goes on to describe, with considerable discomfort, how she went up to two people after the group, warmly letting each of them know that she valued their input, feeling duty bound to behave in a deeply grateful way to anyone who compliments or praises her. These women did not rebuff the patient, but also did not reply "gushingly," as she would have. They did not assure her that her comments were valued. Hope felt humiliated by this, absolutely mortified, and decided that these women didn't want anything to do with her—that they saw her as "bad." She had a hard time keeping herself together after the group.

"Interesting," I reply, "that although these women did not push you away, because they did not reply the way you had hoped, you felt humiliated, as if you had done something bad."

Hope said that this situation reminded her of our last session over three weeks ago. In it she had been complaining about feeling that her patients (she is a therapist herself) were a painful burden, adding that I probably feel that way about my practice too. When I responded that I didn't feel that way about my practice she told me that she had immediately felt two things. First there was tremendous relief that I didn't view *her* as a painful burden. Second, that I was saying that "good" therapists do not feel this way, the way she feels (viewing her patients as burdensome). The implicit comparison was clear. Unlike me, she is not one of the good people. *I replied that it must be draining to feel that good therapists never feel burdened, that in order to feel like a good therapist you shouldn't ever feel burdened.* Hope responded tearily, "No, because I *need* you to take care of me. It's what I *can do* immediately to regain the good feelings—to MAKE UP (she emphasized the words, pointing to the earlier reference to the "makeup" counter) for my badness.

Hope was able to redirect my understanding from the feeling of being burdened to what was emotionally central to her, her conviction about her badness. And I was able to leave my hypothesis about being burdened to follow her emotional lead. Hope's conviction about her badness at this moment is very strong. She needs to feel the badness she is feeling so I can take care of her. Developing more ability to be with and also stand apart from her feelings could be helpful. I asked Hope if she can stand aside from her humiliation and allow herself to have the feelings, she is having without judging them. The image of her father came to my mind and I remembered that her father is generally a loving inner figure for her so I asked her if she can imagine her father understanding her situation in the dream. An echo of the intersection of the dream and her therapy is present. Hope sobs and replies "My father *totally* understood. He wasn't upset at all. He did understand me! *"What then is the heart of these feelings you are having now?"* I ask. Hope moans and covers her face. Crying, she tells me, "I remember climbing into his lap. He's wearing a vest and it has a very silky back that I would touch and feel. I would lean against him while I cried. She is sobbing. I was never ever able to get comfort from anyone but Pop, not my Mother, nor my grandmother . . . .

After Hope has calmed herself, I comment: *"The impulse to make yourself feel humiliated involves getting yourself into a place where you can be comforted by someone who loves you. It was an inspired way of getting what you needed even though feeling awful had to be a part of it."*

Exploring Hope's associations to the dream and her work with me enabled us to develop a better understanding of the pervasiveness of her sense of badness. What we came to understand is that Hope *needed* to feel bad in order to be able to crawl into her father's lap, in order to be comforted by him in the past, and by me in the present. She had an emotional investment in feeling bad. Paradoxically, it helped her to feel better. Rationally working to change her cognitive belief (i.e., focusing on whether she really was bad or not) would not have addressed the core issue because the fundamental dynamic involved *needing* to feel bad in order to get the other's loving concern. Without this, Hope felt alone, depressed and disconnected. The dream points us to an enactment in which Hope unconsciously *uses* feeling bad as a way to connect with a loved one. This enactment is played out with me in the treatment, in her relationships with others and in her relationship to herself.

Understanding the enactment and having compassion for the little girl part of herself that had to develop this way of relating to herself in order to deal with the lack of emotional connection she experienced growing up, allows Hope to develop a different perspective on her pervasive feeling of badness.

Building a narrative that acknowledges the necessity for having, as a child, developed defenses that in the present are experienced only as problems (however attached one has become to them) and developing compassion for these split-off protective aspects of self are essential aspects of healing from trauma.

The therapist has a daunting task: staying with the patient through storms so intense they can reach cyclone proportions and using the calm before and after these storms as opportunities for growth. Pine's (1993) admonition to strike while the iron is cold comes to mind. Essentially, this advice is to use the time before and after emotional triggering as opportunities for developing insight and integration. This is not an easy task. Working with these upheavals can be intense, especially when transference fantasies are at the eye of the storm. Using resistance as a guide can be very helpful. Resistance points directly to the fears and fantasies that need to be uncovered.

Central to the process of change is working on the patient's ability to develop an observing ego, an ability to stand aside and reflect on inner experience. The observing ego is the part of the self that can stand back and allow the other aspects of self—those that are often negative and even terrifying—to be given leave to speak as valued and respected contributors to the therapeutic dialogue. This is a complex task that is not accomplished easily or quickly. Essentially, we are talking about giving recognition to intrapsychic aspects of self, encouraging these often disconnected parts of the self to have a voice.

Therapeutically, asking the patient to actually give voice to these less integrated aspects of self is often valuable. As patients express the voice of these disowned aspects of self (the killer stalking them, the terrifying fears of opening oneself to love, the part that doesn't want to be visible), they get to see the fears and fantasies in a situation where they can interact with them in a more integrated way.

The process of changing our relationship to trauma does not involve a simple cognitive "reframing" of the way we think about the trauma. The heart of trauma is emotional activation at a very intense, brain-driven level. It is not resolved by mental gymnastics or cognitive reframing. Repeating affirmations that you are a good person does not work if, like Hope, there is a need to feel bad. Instead, changing requires engaging (with courage and caring consideration) the depth of emotional relatedness to the self. Without this emotionally based engagement, and the small steps of working through obstacles and attachments, change may be thwarted.

CHAPTER 18

Taking Effective Action

Helping patients identify experiences on the continuum of emotional activation and helping them generate a compassionate narrative that connects past with present are important, but recovering from developmental trauma requires more. Taking effective action is an essential element in the process of any psychological change. It is vital in recovery from complex developmental trauma. New and different action is necessary in order to rewire a brain whose networks are not yet optimized for the way that patients are striving to relate in the present. If the patient does not claim the possibility of effective action as part of his or her strategy for change, the therapeutic process will not be as effective as it could be.

Action is *effective* when it serves the integrated conscious core of the individual—the centered self. Effective action empowers the patient. It counteracts counteracts the learned helplessness that is at the heart of trauma. Emotion evolved to give us a body-based shortcut to mobilize the process of getting our needs met: emotion readies us for expedited action. These emotionally based actions free us from taking extra time to deliberate. In many situations, this organization helps to move us toward what we desire or to keep us out of danger. It can be lifesaving. But emotionally based actions can also get us into trouble when inappropriate early patterns of emotional arousal are triggered by associations in the present. The re-activation of early traumatic experiences is deeply felt and generally accompanied by an unshakable sense of conviction indicating that right-brain dominance has taken hold. Strong emotional conviction can be a signal that integrated mental functioning has weakened or been eclipsed.

Avoidance is one of the tactics that people often employ during traumatic experiences, but avoidant action has to be carefully evaluated to ensure that it serves the person in the present. Avoidance can be problematic if patients develop a reliance on avoidance strategies as a primary mode of relating. Avoiding situations that are reminders of traumatic experiences is not an effective and centered approach; avoidance puts fear in charge. It reinforces the idea that what we are afraid of is objectively threatening in the way it seems to us and that the only way we can take care of ourselves is by running away. Effective action, on the other hand, flows from centered and balanced assessments made through the patient's integrated sense of self. Encouraging this kind of action therapeutically can be as simple as having the patient choose where to sit or what to talk about, or as complex as identifying the patient's wish to assert what he or she wants to do. What is empowering is unique to the patient. Therapists understand that helping patients to take charge of their lives whenever possible can be reparative. We facilitate this when we truly believe that the patient's solutions lie largely within.

In psychodynamic psychotherapy, many of the actions we work on with patients are internal. Often, these actions are not observable from the outside. They include, for example, patients asking themselves to modulate a self-critical voice, risking telling the therapist what they were really thinking, choosing to take a moment to reflect and consider what is going on inside, resisting an urge to demand perfection or to gratify impulses immediately. Effective action often involves differentiating an impulse that is rooted in early defenses from a considered decision that emerges from balanced deliberation. This can be quite difficult, especially since right-brain dominated experience is so often accompanied by intense emotional conviction. Sometimes, patients learn to use the emergence of feelings of conviction or urgency as a clue that the feeling may not be coming from a centered place. Even though they are not readily observable, these are important actions. They involve patients changing how they relate to themselves.

Intrapsychic actions are powerful because of the sheer volume of the opportunities they provide patients to work on changing these modes of relating. Every time patients remind themselves that a punitive mode of relating to themselves is not helpful, they are developing their observing ego capacity as well as working on integration. When a patient notices that a feeling carries a sense of urgency or desperation, and then does not act on it, he is taking the effective action of slowing down the process, an action that preempts or minimizes the power of emotional hijacking. When a patient chooses to tell the therapist a thought or fantasy, going against another part of her that wants to push it away, she is taking effective action. With patients who are on the higher end of the emotional activation continuum, those who have been traumatized, taking effective action is often related to actions that they were not able to take during the original traumatic situation. Having to be silent, to not fight back, to hide the truth, to pretend, to lie to self or others are commonly experienced necessities associated with traumatizing childhood experiences.

Allowing oneself to move into a previously forbidden way of being can be reparative as long as it is done with the support of the integrated self. Frequently, we get notice of the importance of these inner actions through the patient's dreams.

Dreams are rich in latent imagery and traces of the organizational structure of the patient's development. We have spoken about my patient Susan, whose father was very judgmental and demanding. As you will recall, Susan developed a number of defenses to protect herself and to make herself feel better in childhood. Chief among these was a profound disconnection from herself, especially from her feelings and her desires. Susan made herself invisible to herself and the world. Susan is the patient who spent eight months of therapy sessions with her arms folded across her chest, demonstrating in a very physical way her defendedness against looking inward. After that time, however, as we began to work on identifying and exploring her feelings, Susan had the following dream:

> *I am at the top of the driveway to my parent's home in the rural countryside. It is night. Very dark. I am looking down the long driveway toward my home. I can see some lights on in the house. Everything is dark all around it. As I look down at the house I am filled with dread, a fear the likes of which I have never known.* [Susan sucks in her breath just remembering the intensity of the fear.] *I am overwhelmed with terror. I know I cannot go down there. The danger starts to close in on me. I have to get away. I turn around and run away from the house onto a path that leads uphill, into the woods. And there I see a giraffe.*

"A giraffe?" I ask. Interesting, I think. "What comes to mind about a giraffe?" Susan draws a blank at first. Then, like the dawning of a new day, she remembers something.

"When I was a child, my Grandmother gave me a book. It was a custom-made book, all about this giraffe named Susan. And every page was a custom-made story about me! It was all about me! I felt like I was invisible in my family, but in the book, I was there, front and center! The whole book was about me! And I can tell you something else . . . . When I left home, I didn't take that many things. But I did take that book. I have it in my apartment even now."

Being recognized, being visible, was a central longing in Susan's life, even as it was something she was deathly afraid of. We can see from the dream that there is a terrifying danger lurking in the family home, a symbol of her childhood. This may have been the first time that Susan allowed herself to genuinely feel the extent of the fear that had dictated her choices during that time. Looking down at the childhood home that was surrounded by blackness symbolically captures the way she related to herself during this period: the darkness (not being able to see what is going on), the disconnection from feelings other than terror; the loss of self that stopped her from knowing who she was and what she wanted.

Her fear of going toward her childhood home has several dimensions. It points to intense fear of something in her childhood and in her family of origin. But it also directs our attention to an intense fear of her *inner* childhood home, the place where she developed the strategies to deal with the realities of her early emotional life. Susan emphasizes the darkness around her home (it is night, very dark; everything is dark around her home), pointing to the sense that in relation to her childhood, a lot is unknown—even more, that there is something that terrifies her in the darkness. But we see something else in the dream. We see that having named the source of her terror, she chooses not to go there. Avoidance, not confronting her fear, is represented in this choice. But also, we see that Susan takes effective action. She turns herself around and goes the other way, into nature (always a love of Susan's), onto a path into the woods. It is a path that leads uphill—it is difficult and requires effort. And there she finds a story about becoming visible, one that is uniquely her own, a custom-made narrative that is hers and hers alone.

The structure of the dream shows us in rich, evocative imagery the conflict Susan now struggles with as well as the path she chooses to take. Knowing that danger lurks in her childhood way of being, Susan decides to take a different path—one that leads her to her unique self. The dream illuminates the organization of the forces at work in Susan's mind: it shows us her current conflict between maintaining the defenses developed in her childhood that keep her invisible and her desire to grow and reconnect with herself, allowing herself to move toward being seen, by me, by herself, by other people.

The trigger of Susan's terror was activated in the dream by going back to her childhood home, especially the going back that involves allowing herself to see and understand what happened in her childhood and what she did to protect herself from the dangers that she experienced. In the dream, the effective action of moving toward being visible and away from her childhood strategies enables her to find her unique self. Susan didn't need her therapist to *direct* her action. Her effective action was represented in the dream for all to see. But she *did* need me to see the effectiveness of her action, as well as the intensity of her terror. She needed to be visible to me.

When, as children, we faced situations we were helpless to change (an alcoholic father, a loss of love, a neglectful mother, an abusive sibling, the loss of a loved one, etc.), we endured not just moments but often years of living where we had little control over the source of our suffering. But even as tiny children, we acted to do what we could to make our situation better. Because we were so young, with such limited mental and physical resources, the sorts of actions we took, actions that became automatic over time, often do not work with our lives in the present. We did what we could do to make ourselves feel better. We took action that was, in some essential way, effective for us, even when it caused us pain. Effective action in the present keeps in mind *and values* our efforts to take care of ourselves as children. Changing involves nurturing the caring aspects of ourselves. This relating to ourselves with care counterbalances the strategies we developed as children that may move us toward guilt, shame, punishment, aggression or other modes of relating that are less than optimal. Appreciating the way that we persevered as children, often at great cost to ourselves, helps us to connect to the proactive parts of ourselves in the present, and, when necessary, to drag ourselves through early fears, ingrained habits and expectations.

> After the very intense sessions in which Jenny spoke about her despair and her feelings of not wanting to live, her mind began to clear. Instead of submitting to impulses to dissociate by watching TV and using her smartphone, she began to feel a desire to delve into her professional writing and research. Gradually, she began to feel better. When we spoke a few weeks later she was happier than she had been for a long time.
>
> "I discovered that I like paper, not people," she said, half-jokingly. "I really like thinking about theory and writing. It is a better way to dissociate!"

I responded that I could see very clearly that she was feeling better. "You have found a way to reconnect with parts of yourself that you had cut off." Jenny responded that she realizes now that one of the reasons she married her husband was because he also loves to write and she finds this connecting and very appealing.

Jenny's ability to fully share the depth of her despair with me was part of what enabled her to take the effective action of stepping back from her childhood hopelessness. Although disconnecting was still an important part of her functioning, Jenny found a way of doing it that worked much better for her. Jenny's issues were not magically resolved but in future sessions she was able to more deeply connect with her inner life. Jenny was able to openly speak with me about being late, which we connected to feelings that I was getting too close. These feelings gave rise to fantasies of ending the treatment. Here we see that Jenny both enacted an impulse to cut herself off (from me, her development and herself) by choosing to be late for our sessions and was able to take the effective action of talking to me about her feelings.

Jenny's newer iteration of her childhood strategy still involves disconnecting but it is, paradoxically, a disconnecting that also involves connecting to herself, her husband, and to me. In later sessions, Jenny was able to explore what she called the heart of the problem: connecting to and loving herself. She works on this every day. Jenny still had impulses to disconnect, but her desire to connect to herself in a loving way combined with the work she is doing enables her to temper those impulses from a more integrated inner place.

There is no way of defining the limits of effective action. Effective actions are any kind of actions that patients take to consolidate the reorganization that they are making in psychotherapy. But we cannot expect effective actions to be without conflict. The inner meaning of taking effective action for the patient must be explored and understood. This inner meaning can be connected to fantasies and feelings that obstruct therapeutic progress. During the course of our exploration, we typically find that patients often have ambivalent reactions to the need to take effective action.

Transference fantasy activity, in relation to the therapeutic process, is always involved with obstacles to moving forward. Inevitably, these transference fantasies organize the patient's wishes and fears about the therapist and are enacted in the process. Fantasies of the therapist giving patients what they want and need are very common. These wishes to have what would amount to effective action coming from the therapist rather than the patient can be very compelling for both parties. Countertransferential pressures to comply with the patient's desire to act out these wishes rather than to explore them can keep the patient in a halfway house between new life and clinging to the past. It may develop that the idea of having to take effective action in one's own behalf, rather than it being given by the therapist, is imbued with the fantasy of not being loved. Acting in one's own behalf then becomes an admission of failure or of not being good enough, not being loveable. It is no wonder that there are inhibitions against taking action for oneself. If the meaning of initiating action involves accepting a belief that we are not valued, standing with our inner voice becomes much more complex. Problems with taking effective action, such as passivity or confusion, may emerge as the way the patient can stimulate and gratify long lost wishes to be taken care of or to involve the therapist in some other way. Working with the fantasies and expectations in the transference is invaluable in these circumstances. Identifying and exploring the obstacles to taking effective action deepens the treatment.

Effective action needs to come from the patient. It cannot be directed by the therapist. Only the patient can know which actions work for them, and they can genuinely know this only after the fact. When they are leading the process, they are regaining a sense of control. This is why noticing the process with the patient and making observations is such a central part of therapeutic action. Our helping patients to notice something enables *them* to actively connect the dots. The following vignette illustrates how subtle this process can be. I return to my work with Marsha—a patient spoken about earlier in the sections on reflections of feeling, meaning and organization—for a more extended example of taking effective action.

Marsha calls in for her session because she is debilitated from various injuries and has been in a wheelchair for a number of years. Her husband is twenty years older than she and has developed dementia. All of his health care falls on her shoulders as his sons (her stepsons) are not in the area. Although physically debilitated, Marsha is a very competent and capable professional. She has cared for her husband for a number of years, making the many medical decisions with wisdom, compassion and ability. When she calls today, however, she is in a panic. Her husband's mental functioning has been declining, so that he is no longer able to collaborate with her in making vital health decisions. *"I'm totally responsible for him now and it's a life and death situation! If I make the wrong decision he could die! This is life and death! I'm so anxious I don't know what to do, but this feeling is going to kill me and then he will be all alone. . . . I'm so alone now. I feel like I am all by myself on a faraway planet and the nearest person is a million miles away. I am a physical wreck!"*

Even though I am right here, attentive and concerned, the power of her emotional triggering doesn't allow her to take in that I am there for her. Emotionally, she is feeling lost, abandoned, hopeless, and helpless in her situation. Marsha's situation *has* changed. She tells me that she has dealt well with her husband's health issues previously, manifesting only moderate amounts of anxiety, but now her emotional arousal is extreme. Marsha is on another planet. She has been emotionally triggered. Right-brain dominated emotional activation has taken control of her experience. Her ability to regulate herself has been com-promised. There is a therapeutic challenge here. On the one hand we want to respect the patient's experience, to stay with the patient but not to the point of over-identifying with that experience (her panic, in this instance). Patients need support for experiencing feelings that they may have spent years denying. On the other hand, we know that Marsha has become emotionally triggered and we want to help her to return to a less triggered, more integrated inner state, *if we can*. (Sometimes that option is not on the table and we need to ride out the emotional storm until an open-ing emerges.) Balancing these concerns is difficult since there are no hard and fast rules to determine with which component we should side at any given moment.

The therapist needs to use all modes of listening to self and other.

This involves connecting with the patient's history, pre-vious sessions and inner conflicts as well as our own countertransferential pushes and pulls. It is often a hard call. I decided that the therapeutic goal with Marsha, for the moment, should be to help her to return to a steadier state, to a state in which she would have more access to integrated functioning instead of remaining a captive of her emotional arousal. The steps of identifying the emotional trigger and establishing a narrative are crucial in helping Marsha to return to a more integrated state, one where she has the possibility of regulating the emotion arousal that is threatening her stability. If we are to listen to Pine's (1993) advice to "strike while the iron is cold," the first thing we need to do is to help her to de-escalate her intense emotional activation.

How do we do this? Let me say a few words about what I am not going to do. I am not going to feed the beast of her hopeless, helpless feelings by over-empathizing with her panic. She is already allowing these feelings and fantasies to dominate her experience. I do want to allow the "hot iron" to cool down, to help her to have the perspective on what is happening come from a more integrated state rather than an archaic, emotionally dominated one. I also want to help her identify the trigger, the stimulus for the emotional arousal that took control of her experience. What did I do? I chose to ask her about the difference between her anxiety in making these health decisions now and when she was making them before and not feeling excessively anxious. I didn't dream up this intervention. *I followed the patient.* Marsha herself mentioned this during the session as she was describing her experience. What I did was to connect with the observation she had already made, and that had been in the background of her experience. But I was asking her instead to bring it to the center of her attention.

It is a small and very common therapeutic action to take seriously what patients say and to ask them to elaborate. By herself, Marsha was not reflecting on her observation. The way she began her session in a state of panic made that very clear. She needed me, that is, the therapeutic process, to ask her to reflect, to take that action. Asking her to examine her process, to reflect on what happened to produce her panic engages her observing ego, another part of her brain. Marsha responded, *"It's the aloneness! He was with me before. Now he's gone and I'm totally alone! Totally responsible. And there's no one to help me. I feel like I'm on another planet totally alone!"*

Her reflecting here is a small step. But it is a very important one. Small steps are powerful and filled with opportunity. Marsha is still very emotionally activated. But in addition, she is also looking at what caused this arousal. This is movement. This is the kind of small movement on which growth depends. Marsha's reflection moves her from thinking about what she cannot control (her husband's growing dementia), toward something she *can* control: her *relationship* to the terrorizing feelings of aloneness that activate childhood feelings, memories and enactments.

I respond, *"So, what gets you into this super anxious state is feeling so isolated and alone . . . like you felt as a very young child with your mother."*

I was able to add the final part of this intervention because it was something that Marsha and I had been working on. Here I was building a narrative connection between the intensity of Marsha's emotional arousal and the terror she felt as a child when her mother disconnected from her. This observation did not magically transform Marsha's experience. Initially, in fact, she returned to her fear, pointing again to how now her situation *was* really a matter of life and death. But as we explored the heart of her arousal, as we "befriended" the feelings she had as a child, she felt the connection. She could imagine how it felt to her like a matter of life and death when her mother was enraged at her, or when her mother gave her the silent treatment. Marsha was regaining more observing ego functions, and as she did, her panic subsided. *She took the effective action of allowing herself to observe her experience at a distance.*

Marsha took the effective action in the session of allowing herself to separate from herself as an endangered and terrified child. These internal (intrapsychic) actions can be very difficult and can require months, if not years of work. The process requires taking tiny steps in exploring the triggers, understanding the defenses put into place, and investigating the investments the patient has in perpetuating maladaptive behaviors. While internal modes of taking effective action are most common in therapy, we must not lose sight of the fact that other modes of taking action are useful, if not necessary, to patients. Sometimes, effective action involves actions the patient takes in the external world. These actions too can be extremely varied. People with and without trauma backgrounds have found help in therapies that involve bodily movement and awareness, group work, yoga, mindfulness, interactions with others, and a host of other experiences that engage a reflective approach to experience. What these approaches have in common is an intention and practice that is grounded in and consolidates an integrated sense of self and a mind-set that encourages the use of observing ego functions. Patients can generate actions that help them resist the pull back into earlier modes of relating and that can keep them in a more balanced state. Essentially, we are helping patients transform their desire to protect themselves through automatic and unconscious actions into a desire for conscious deliberative acts that protect themselves in ways that work better for them in the present. It is especially important to keep in mind that these actions take many forms and typically involve very small steps. Change lives in small steps.

As therapists, we are trained to collaborate and explore with patients the options that emerge in the course of treatment. We listen to how they examine their choices in relation to their integrative functioning. We are especially tuned into how unconscious impulses may emerge and displace more integrative organization. We also listen for what is being avoided or pushed away. We use the collaborative nature of our relationship to explore choices that feel effective.

We must not forget that effective action is action that works for the patient. These actions can be taken as part of the therapeutic process, in relation to the patients themselves, or they can involve the patient's action in the outer world. One of the findings of research on psychodynamic psychotherapy is that not only does psychodynamic treatment have a significant effect (Shedler, 2010), meaning that it has been scientifically demonstrated to be effective, but also that the benefits of psychodynamic psychotherapy increase over time, after treatment is terminated (Abbass et al., 2006; Anderson & Lambert, 1995; de Maat et al., 2009; Leichsenring & Rabung, 2008; Leichsenring et al., 2004). Learning how to take effective action in the context of new understandings of oneself is an important aspect of this remarkable consequence of psychodynamic therapy.

Susan, my patient, struggled for years against impulses to cut herself off, in part because having others direct her made her feel taken care of. She was having friends over for a warm winter lunch in front of her fire in the city. She pulled the chicken pot pie out of the oven and tasted it. It was a tad soft, not quite as crispy as she would have liked. Her initial reaction was, "Too bad, it could have been a little better." But then, as she was socializing with her guests and her partner, she began to reflect. "What am I waiting for?" she asked herself. "Someone else to come and do it right, make it better?" It took a little while to reclaim her own power, but after a few minutes Susan decided that she could make this work. She excused herself, put the pie back into the oven and was able to serve her pot pie crisp the way she wanted it. This was a small step but a very effective action in how it signified her triumphing over an unquestioned assumption that she had to endure what she was given. Susan's action expanded her personal agency.

Working with our patients to help them understand themselves better and through this understanding to make better life choices, we rejoice in their ability to take effective action in any part of their lives. As we see patients enabling themselves to stand with themselves, doing what works for them with balanced conscious deliberation, we are seeing change at work. The breakthrough nature of effective action can combine new ways of relating to the self with a statement in the outer world, integrating inner therapeutic work with proactive engagement in external reality.

Barbara was divorced from her high-powered husband after thirty-five years of marriage. During her marriage, Barbara had prioritized her family life over her writing career, raising two children with whom she had close, gratifying relationships. She had depended on her husband in many ways during their long relationship, and she was anxious in the uncertainties of her new situation and about being able to make it on her own. Would she be able to find a place to live, develop a new life for herself, deal with the losses she now had to endure? Barbara started by being her own advocate in her divorce. She went on to describe taking an action that symbolized her ability to reshape her life:

> A few months after my divorce, at the age of 70, I did something I thought I'd never do: I got a tattoo. I'd grown up in an era when the only people who got tattoos were bikers and sailors. Yet there I was, an elderly woman who used proper grammar and dressed her age, following suit. My friends thought I was out if my mind, and in a way they were right. At the time, I felt utterly raw and fearful, facing what looked to me like an unbearably lonely future. In that state, I found the idea of doing something preposterously out-of-character immensely appealing.
>
> Which is why I now sport—on my neck, just behind my right ear—the image of a small crescent moon cradling two stars. The latter represent my son and daughter, the living products of my marriage. And in the weeks after having their symbolic presence engraved on my skin, I felt my feelings of loss ebbing away. In fact, those two tiny stars became a daily reminder of what I *hadn't* lost, as well as proof positive that the thirty-five years I spent with their father hadn't been a complete waste of time. Although I didn't know it at the time, I realize now that having the moon and the stars inked indelibly into my skin signified my determination to reshape a relevant life, one complete with joy and purpose.

Barbara took an action that carried forward and symbolized her courage and determination to remake her life. Effective actions, whether internal or expressed in the world, carry meanings that are always powerful. Their rich symbolic aspect can be a substantive part of the healing process.

Our journey has come full circle. We have explored a challenging terrain with the tools of psychodynamic psychotherapy — the attitudes, skills and modes of relating that enable us to map the landscape of the mind. Our adventure has introduced us to inspiring struggles that actual people have generously shared on their own voyages of discovery. Through their unique experiences, we have developed a fuller appreciation of the common features that make therapy effective: the importance of creating a safe harbor where patients can plumb the depths of their darkest secrets; the centrality of the collaborative nature of this work, work that cannot be accomplished alone; the value of a psychodynamic frame that holds the treatment; the necessity of connecting past and present; the importance of "thinking small" as we look for signs of emotional triggering and contemplate effective actions. Above all, we have developed an ability to listen for the many layers of meaning, organization and symbolic resonance in the multifaceted communications expressed through the feelings, fantasies and actions of both participants. Not only does this adventure have no equal, but it also enriches the lives of those who choose to engage it.

References

Abbass, A. A., Hancock, J. T., Henderson, J., and Kisely, S. (2006). Short-term psychodynamic psychotherapies for common mental disorders. Cochrane Database of Systematic Reviews, Issue 4, Article No. CD004687. doi: 10.1002/14651858.CD004687.pub3

Abend, S. M. (1986). Countertransference, empathy and the analytic ideal: The impact of life stresses on analytic capability. *Psychoanal Q.,* 55:563–575.

Adler, E. and Bachant, J. (1998). *Working in depth: A clinician's guide to framework and flexibility in the analytic relationship.* Northvale, New Jersey and London England: Jason Aronson Inc.

Anderson, E. M. and Lambert, M. J. (1995). Short-term dynamically oriented psychotherapy: A review and meta-analysis. *Clinical Psychology Review,* 15, 503–514. doi: 10.1016/0272-7358(95)00027-M

Arlow, J. A. (1969). Unconscious fantasy and disturbances of conscious experience. *Psychoanalytic Quarterly,* 38:1–27.

Bachant, J. and Adler, E. (1997). Transference: co-constructed or brought to the interaction? *Journal of the American Psychoanalytic Association,* 45:1097–1120.

Beres, D. and Arlow, J. A. (1974). Fantasy and Identification in Empathy. *Psychoanal Q.,* 43:26–50.

Brenner, C. (1982). *The Mind in Conflict*. New York: International Universities Press.

Browning, M. (2019). Our Symbolic minds: What are they really? *Psychoanalytic Quarterly,* 88(1):25–52. doi: 10.1080/00332828.2019. 1556037

Busch, F. (2014). *Creating a Psychoanalytic mind: A Psychoanalytic method and theory.* London and New York: Routledge.

Borrell-Carrio, F., Suchman, A. L., and Epstein, R. M. (2004). The Biopsychosocial Model 25 Years Later: Principles, Practice, and Scientific Inquiry. *Ann. Fam. Med.,* 2(6):576–582. doi: 10.1370/afm.245

Clyman, R. B. (1991). The procedural organization of emotions: A contribution from cognitive science to the psychoanalytic theory of therapeutic action. *J. Am. Psychoanal. Assoc.,* 39S:349–382.

Cozolino, L. (2002). *The neuroscience of psychotherapy.* New York: W.W. Norton & Co.

———. (2006). *The neuroscience of human relationships: attachment and the developing social brain.* New York: W.W. Norton & Co.

Damasio, A. (1994). Descartes Error: Emotion, reason and the human brain. New York: Grosset/Putnam.

———. (1999). The Feeling of what happens: Body and emotion in the making of consciousness. New York: Harcourt Brace.

———. (2003). Looking for Spinoza: Joy, sorrow, and the feeling brain. New York and London: Harcourt.

Deacon, T. W. (1997). *The Symbolic Species: The co-evolution of language and the brain.* New York and London: W.W. Norton& Company.

de Maat, S., de Jonghe, F., Schoevers, R., and Dekker, J. (2009). The effectiveness of long-term psychoanalytic therapy: A systematic review of empirical studies. *Harvard Review of Psychiatry,* 17:1–23. doi: 10.1080/16073220902742476

Edelman, G. M. (2004). *Wider than the sky: the phenomenal gift of consciousness*. New Haven and London: Yale University Press.

Ellman, P. and Goodman, N. (2017). (Eds.) *Finding unconscious fantasy in narrative, trauma, and body pain: a clinical guide*. London and New York: Routledge.

Faulkner, W. (1951). *Requiem for a Nun*. New York: Random House.

Fenichel, O. (1941). *Problems of psychoanalytic technique*. Trans. D. Brunswick. New York: Psychoanalytic Quarterly.

Freud, S. (1900). The Interpretation of dreams. *Standard Edition:* 4/5:1–626.

———. (1905). Fragment of an analysis of a case of hysteria. Vol. VII, *Standard Edition*.

———. (1912). The dynamics of transference. Standard Edition: 12:99–108.

———. (1914). Remembering, repeating and working through. *Standard Edition,* 13:145–156.

———. (1937). Analysis terminable and interminable. *Standard Edition,* 23:216–253.

Ginot, E. (2015). *The Neuropsychology of the Unconscious: Integrating brain and mind in psychotherapy*. Norton: New York and London.

———. (2019). Personal communication.

Goodman, N. (2017). The finding theater: a schema for finding unconscious fantasy. In Finding Unconscious fantasy in narrative, trauma and body pain. London and New York: Routledge.

Goulding, R. A. and Schwartz, R. C. (1995). *The Mosaic Mind: Empowering the Tormented Selves of Child Abuse Survivors*. New York: Norton.

Greenson, R. R. (1968). *The Technique and practice of psychoanalysis*. New York: International Universities Press.

Grossman, W. (1992). Comments on the concept of the 'Analyzing Instrument'. *Journal of Clinical Psychoanalysis,* 2:261–71.

Herman, J. (1992/1997/2015). *Trauma and Recovery*. New York: Basic Books.

Howell, E. F. (2005). *The Dissociative Mind*. Hillsdale, NJ: Analytic Press.

Isaacs, S. (1952). The nature and function of phantasy. In J. Riviere (Ed.), *Developments of psychoanalysis* (pp. 62–121). London, Hogarth Press.

James, R. K. (2008). *Crisis Intervention Strategies*. Belmont, CA: Brooks/Cole.

Kohut, H. (1971). *The Analysis of the self*. New York: International Universities Press.

——. (1982). *The Restoration of the self*. New York: International Universities Press.

Langer, S. (1953). *Feeling and form*. New York: Charles Scribner & Sons.

——. (1967). *Mind: An Essay on Human Feeling*. Vol. 1. Baltimore: Johns Hopkins Univ. Press.

——. (1988). *Mind: An Essay on Human Feeling* (Van Den Heuvel G. abridger). Baltimore: Johns Hopkins Univ. Press.

Langs, R. (1975). *International Journal of Psychoanalytic Psychotherapy* 4:106–141.

LeDoux, J. (1998). *The Emotional Brain: The Mysterious underpinnings of emotional life*. New York: Touchstone/Simon and Schuster.

Leichsenring, F. and Rabung, S. (2008). Effectiveness of long-term psychodynamic psychotherapy: A meta-analysis. *Journal of the American Medical Association*, 300:1551–1565.

Leichsenring, F., Rabung, S., and Leibing, E. (2004). The efficacy of short-term psychodynamic psychotherapy in specific psychiatric disorders: A meta-analysis. *Archives of General Psychiatry*, 61:1208–1216.

Levin, J. (2018). Personal communication.

Loving Vincent. (2017). Dorota Kobiela and Hugh Welchman, directors. Docudrama.

Lynch, A. A., Bachant, J. L., and Richards, A. D. (1998). A Spectrum of Interaction. Panel Presentation at The American Psychoanalytic Annual Meeting. Toronto, Canada.

Lynch, A. A. (2018). Personal communication.

Merriam-Webster Online (n.d.). In *Merriam Webster Online*, Retrieved September 24, 2016, from http://www.merriam-webster.com/dictionary/attitude.

Orange, D. M. (1995). *Emotional Understanding: Studies in Psychoanalytic epistemology*. New York and London: The Guilford Press.

Panksepp, J. (1998). *Affective Neuroscience: the foundations of human and animal emotions*. New York and Oxford: Oxford University Press.

Pine, F. (1993). A contribution to the analysis of the psychoanalytic process. *Psychoanalytic Quarterly, 62*:185–205.

Rangell, L. (1983). Defense and resistance in psychoanalysis and life. *Journal of the American Psychoanalytic Association*, 31(Suppl.): 147–174.

Richards, A. D. (2005). Personal communication.

Sacks, O. (1985). *The man who mistook his wife for a hat and other clinical tales*. New York: Simon and Schuster.

Schafer, R. (1959). Generative empathy in the treatment situation. *Psychoanalytic Quarterly*, 28:345.

Schore, A. N. (2011). *The science of the art of psychotherapy*. New York: Norton.

———. (2015). Foreword. In Ginot, E. *The Neuropsychology of the Unconscious: Integrating brain and mind in psychotherapy*. Norton: New York and London.

Shapiro, T. (1981). Empathy: A critical revaluation. 1(3):423–488.

Shedler, J. (2010). The Efficacy of psychodynamic psychotherapy. *American Psychologist*, 65(2):98–109. doi: 10.1037/a0018378

Smith, S. (1977). The golden fantasy: a regressive reaction to separation anxiety. *International Journal of Psycho-Analysis*, 58:311–324.

Solms, M. (2003). Do unconscious phantasies really exist? In Riccardo Steiner, (Ed.), *Unconscious Phantasy*, Chapter 3, 99–115. London: Karnac.

———. (2013). The conscious id. *Neuropsychoanalysis*, 15:5–19.

Solms, M. and Panksepp, J. (2012). The "id" knows more than the "ego" admits: neuropsychoanalytic and primary consciousness perspectives on the interface between affective and cognitive neuroscience. *Brain Science,* 2:147–75.

Solms, M. and Turnbull, O. (2002). *The Brain and the Inner world: An introduction to the neuroscience of subjective experience.* New York: Other Press.

Stefánsson, H. (2007). The biology of behaviour: scientific and ethical implications. *EMBO Reports,* 8(Suppl 1):S1–S2. http://doi.org/10.1038/sj.embor.7401012.

Stolorow, R. and Lachman, F. (1984/1985). Transference: the future of an illusion. *Annual of Psychoanalysis,* 12/13:19–37.

Van der Kolk, B. (2005). Developmental trauma disorder. *Psychiatric Annals,* (35:5):401–408.

——. (2013). Frontiers of Trauma Treatment. Workshop at Cape Cod Institute, Eastham, MA.

——. (2014). *The Body keeps the score: Brain, mind, and body in the healing of trauma.* New York: Viking.

Viorst, J. (1998). *Necessary losses: The Loves Illusions Dependencies and Impossible Expectations That All of us Have.* New York: Simon Schuster.

Waelder, R. (1936). The Principle of Multiple Function. *Psychoanalytic Quarterly,* 5:45–62; reprint: 2007, 76:75–92.

Young, M. E. (2006). *Learning the art of helping.* Upper Saddle River, NJ: Merrill/Prentice Hall.

Zwiebel, R. (2004). The third position: Reflection about internal analytic working process. *Psychoanalytic Quarterly,* 73:215–65.

CPSIA information can be obtained
at www.ICGtesting.com
Printed in the USA
BVHW040832171119
564070BV00018B/766/P

9 781949 093360